Dedicated to Paramedics and EMTs,
past, present, and future;
giving of themselves in the service of
others.

And then I cried…
A Paramedic's Diary

ISBN 978-1514634622
Printed in the United States of America

And then I cried...

A Paramedic's Diary

By Lance Hodge

Contents

Introduction

Some would say I spent 13 years as a *hero*. None of us thought of ourselves that way, and even now, and with the realizations I've gained only after being away from it, I'm still uncomfortable thinking of what I did as heroic, it certainly wasn't heroic in the *military* sense. But in many ways it was, and I'll say that now, not so much for me but for all of those who are doing that job now. Our EMT's and Paramedics regularly put themselves in dangerous, even life-threatening situations to do what they do. Some would say it's heroic, fine.

The Job of a paramedic is unique. Few occupations allow you to be the one to "save the day" every time you go to work. But it is a *job* and when you're in it you tend to see it that way, as just a job. The events which compete for the evening news are routine to you. A paramedic might stop the flow of blood from a gunshot wound, and then, an hour later, deliver a baby. Ten minutes after eating an English muffin at the fire station you could be lying on your back in spilled gasoline trying to pull someone from the tangled wreckage of his car.

So ask a paramedic if he or she is a hero, and they'll tell you it's *just their job*. They don't know yet, they're too close to it, it's too routine, and they just don't see it.

I spent 13 years as a paramedic with the *Los Angeles City Fire Department*. This book is dedicated to all those heroes who race to help when you call. To the fire fighters and police, to the EMT's and Paramedics, who work each day in a job that is never routine, who give more of themselves than they yet know.

You don't hear "Thank you" that often as a paramedic. It's hard for the patient to think of that during an emergency, but that was just fine with me. It was a privilege just to have that *job*. I was a *Paramedic*, and thinking of it now something of an Angel to hundreds of people who needed me.

I felt it then, but can see *now* more clearly, how special that was. The pages that follow are reflections on a career in EMS. They are the images that come sweetly with smiles, and that lay deep inside quietly haunting me.

I have no choice but to call it a *diary*. These pages come from years of memories, from a real life touched by so many others. I've changed names and places enough to obscure most of those who shared these moments with me, but they are *real* moments, *real* people, *real* tragedies, and *real* joys. My goal in writing this was to smile at remembering, and to finally cry, remembering too much.

If you feel more mortal after reading this, and take better care to be safe and healthy, then I have accomplished something wonderful. If you have a better understanding of the people who race by you with lights and sirens blaring after reading this book, then I have done a service to you and to them.

To all the patients who I could help, I'm glad I was there for you. To all of those who I could not help, I hope there is a Heaven. I tried my best to be your Angel.

Lance Hodge

Some vocabulary...

EMT: *Emergency Medical Technician.* The basic level of medical training for firefighters and those who work on ambulances. The EMT is trained in 'Basic Life Support' (BLS) and basic medical skills as opposed to 'Advanced Life Support' (ALS) which Paramedics provide.

Paramedic: Paramedics have the same training as EMT's but then undergo additional training that allows them to do certain advanced procedures, start IV's, give dozens of medications, interpret EKG's and use 'Advanced airways' such as Endotracheal Tubes.

EMS: *Emergency Medical Services.* Your local EMS system may use EMT's or Paramedics or a combination of the two. May be delivered by a fire department or private company or both.

OCD: *Operations Control Division.* The L.A. City Fire Department dispatch center.

Biocom: The original name for the radio communication device used by Paramedics to contact their Base Station Hospital.

Base Station Hospital: The hospital assigned to a particular EMS unit. They may provide some restocking of supplies for units assigned to them, and are generally the hospital the assigned EMT's or Paramedics will contact to 'call in' their patient's signs and symptoms. Such contact may be required to receive 'orders' to administer certain medications.

Backboard: A long plastic board used to immobilize the spine in suspected neck and back injury.

PA: Public address system. In fire stations to broadcast a message throughout the entire station.

Ambu-bag/Bag-Valve-Mask Device (BVM): Bag/Mask device used to give artificial breathing to a patient by squeezing a bag.

Incident number: The number assigned to each call. Generally, the number of calls in a 24 hour period beginning at midnight.

Brady: (Bradycardia) pulse less than 60/minute.

Tachy: (Tachycardia) pulse faster than 100/minute.

Defibrillator: (**AED**) *Automated Electronic Defibrillator*. Paramedics generally use a 'manual' defibrillator which offers more functions controlled by the Paramedic. EMT's generally use the AED which is mostly 'automatic' and requires little training to use. Both types of defibrillators *'stop the heart'* to wipe out *Ventricular Fibrillation* (quivering not pumping of the heart) and then the heart *may* begin a functional beat.

Peds: *Pediatric*. Children.

Auto-ped: Vehicle vs. Pedestrian.

Full arrest: 'Full' meaning *respiratory* and *cardiac* arrest (no breathing and no pulse) You can have *Respiratory Arrest* alone which is no breathing but they *do* have a pulse.

I.C.U: Intensive Care Unit

Stat Ident: 'Hospital slang' for hurry up and get identification/information on the patient. Name, address, insurance info.

Rescue: Or **RA** (Rescue Ambulance) L.A. City Fire Dept. designation for a fire department ambulance. May be staffed with EMT's, Paramedics, or a mixture.

PD: Police Department.

Engine: Engine Company. The smaller firetruck, generally a 'pump' with hoses and miscellaneous equipment. Staffed with several firefighters (Captain, Engineer, Firefighters)

C-Spine: 'Cervical' spine. The term c-spine precautions means to immobilize the entire spine, usually using a cervical collar, a *long back board,* and straps.

Stokes basket: A basket-type stretcher. The thing you may see someone strapped in while hanging from a helicopter or being pulled up or lowered down with a winch.

Streamlight: A brand of flashlight, mine was metal and five cells, and BRIGHT.

Sick: Nebulous dispatch designation meaning someone is 'sick' (something wrong) but no specifics as to what the medical problem might be.

Man-down: Nebulous dispatch designation meaning somebody is reported as being on the ground, usually unknown why.

Normal Saline: 0.9% Saline solution for IV replacement of lost blood volume.

D5W: An IV solution to run very slowly (**TKO**) *To Keep Open,* just to prevent the IV catheter from clotting, used as a 'life line' to administer medications if needed. Often started *prophylactically* "Just in case" it's needed.

Maxi-drip: IV tubing usually used with **Normal Saline** IV, to give fluids rapidly if needed (blood loss, shock)

Mini-drip: IV tubing usually used with a D5W IV, small opening for TKO IV, can't administer fluid rapidly (for medical problems not trauma)

Pole hole: The hole in the ceiling to slide 'the pole' from the upper floors.

Bucketing: Dumping water on someone at the fire station, for fun, generally a 'no-no' these days.

MAST: *Military Anti-Shock Trousers.* A nylon suit with Velcro to wrap around a patient's legs and abdomen. A foot pump inflates the suit around the body like a blood pressure cuff. Raises blood pressure and stabilizes massive fractures of legs and pelvis. Not used in Los Angeles County for many years.

Sublingual: Under the tongue. Nitroglycerine is given there.

Lidocaine: Can reduce the chance of *Ventricular Fibrillation* occurring or reoccurring.

Bolus: An injection of a medication.

Epi: Epinephrine/Adrenalin. Can stimulate the heart to beat, can be used for allergic reactions.

Atropine: Drug that can speed up the heart.

Sinus: The normal 'pacemaker' node in the heart.

Unifocal (PVC's): An abnormal heartbeat coming from the same source/node.

Multifocal (PVC's): Abnormal heartbeat coming from various nodes, generally more dangerous.

PVC: *Premature Ventricular Contraction.* Potentially dangerous heart *arrhythmia* (abnormal 'skipped' heart beat)

M.S.: Can mean *Morphine Sulfate* (Morphine). Used to reduce chest pain from Myocardial Infarction.

M.I.: *Myocardial Infarction* = Heart Attack. Death of heart tissue (Myocardium)

'C' Booth: Was one of the main trauma areas at County USC (University of Southern California) Medical Center Trauma Center.

Johnny and Roy: The stars of "**Emergency**" a fake 'reality' show from the 70's that largely introduced the world to 'modern' EMS and the distinction between EMT's and Paramedics.

Nystagmus: Rapid twitching of the eyes from side-to-side, can indicate PCP use and/or alcohol use.

White box: This was a small 'trauma kit' that held mostly bandages and a blood pressure cuff. We could grab that for simple injuries instead of the 'big box' with medications and IV supplies.

The Red Book: We kept our run reports in a large red notebook/folder, and generally carried this folder with us to every call. An 'EMS report' was filled out for every call.

Note:

There's a *lingo* in my fire department, and it's not the same everywhere. Let's say you work at Station 46; another Paramedic asks you where you work, and you'd say "46's." We don't generally say "Station 46" or "46." It's 38's, 82's, 15's, 13's, 66's, etc. So that's how it's written in this book, and unless you knew that you might wonder what that's all about. Now here we go…

Chapter One
To talk to the ducks

We were all talking about the big game. Kareem was talking about retirement, and two blocks away Tommy's mother was talking to her friend on the phone.

Tommy loved to talk to the ducks. I'll bet it was that big white one Tommy saw that morning. Tommy was full of adventure at three years old, and fearless.

"What time is the game?" I asked.

"It's at seven, we'll let you know who won" one of the firemen said, smiling.

I turned to Jack, he already had that disgusted look, the one that says, "Yup, we'll probably be out running calls" without saying it. The paper said it was probably Kareem's last season.

Tommy's mother was a good mother, she checked on Tommy every couple of minutes, especially when he was playing on the patio deck. She had told Tommy how dangerous the canal was and to never, ever, go close unless Mommy was with him.

Tommy was such a big boy. Only three, but I could tell by the way he was dressed that morning that 'he' was sure he was a "big boy."

"We've got a backboard out at Marina and we need to pick up a couple bags of normal saline" Jack said.

"Yeah, let's get that done this morning." I didn't want any projects to get in the way in case we *were* around at game time.

The voice over the PA blasted into the kitchen. "Wally-ball, Wally-ball... on the court in one minute, Wally-ball." From across the kitchen table one of the Firemen couldn't resist. "You guys better change your rotation, or maybe you could play wearing stilts. Maybe you could spike the ball then." He laughed, and I gave him a dirty look. Then I said something to imply that he was gay, his wrist went limp and he said, "Who told you?" It was the standard banter, before *Political Correctness* was mandated. Actually, it was a little more subdued than normal, maybe it was the weather. It looked like it could rain, of course in the morning next to the beach you never really knew.

Tommy had his little red jacket on with his hood pulled up and snug around his face, and was wearing his white high tops. I wonder if he had ever seen Kareem play?

"Awwrrright, nice hit" Jack shouted.
It was an awesome spike. "Eat leather!" I yelled.
"14-6" proclaimed Tony from across the net.
"14-6? You had five!" Jack complained.
"No way" Tony insisted.
Jack cleared his throat. "It was 12-4. You served it into the net. We slammed that one off Captain Brennen's head, and then you netted. Warren served it into the wall, it was your serve, you got a point when Vince stepped over the line on Larry's foot, then Carlos dinked it over Ed, then we just killed it. 14-5."
None of us knew if it was the right score, but the recap was a thing of beauty. 14-5.

Tommy's mother found him. He was floating in the canal. "Tommy!" She jumped in and pulled him up on her neighbor's small boat dock. The canal was shallow; she was standing up in the water. She screamed, just "Help!" over and over.
Her neighbor opened the patio door and ran toward them. Tommy's mother looked up at her, "Call the Paramedics,

hurry!" The neighbor turned and screamed to her husband.

Tommy's mother started to breathe into his mouth. It was all too much like a movie; it seems that way sometimes, like a movie.

"O.K we're warmed up, one more game."

"A coke game. I'll take Dr.Pepper" I said, as I tossed them the ball. "Loser serves" I said with a smile.

The speaker in the court bellowed, "Rescue 63, Engine 63, a drowning. 426 Canal Court, time out 0735, incident number 79, OCD clear."

We were out of the station in less than a minute. We parked the ambulance a minute later and I could see them about four houses away. "It's a kid" I said. "Over there on that dock."

"I'll get the peds Ambu-bag" Jack said. We had to run down a small walkway along the canal. I remember saying "Damn" as I got closer. Jack was right behind me and the guys from the Engine Company were right behind him.

He was so cute. He was just perfect. Those little tennis shoes, the tiny size Levi's, and his nice warm red Jacket with the hood all snugged up.

His mother looked up at me, stunned. I said, "O. K, we're here, let me do that."

I asked her how long he had been in the water. She said she couldn't find him anywhere. I asked her how long he had been gone. "Only a few minutes. I was on the phone."

I picked him up. His lips were blue and cold on mine.

"Let's go! We need a driver to Marina."

"I'll drive!" yelled Warren.

"And another guy in the back" I said, between breaths.

"I'll go" shouted Carlos.

I turned toward the ambulance. A man came around the corner at the same time, and paused for a second; he looked down at the boy. "Tommy" he said. The man had a look on his face as if *he* were dying and those were his last words. Somebody behind me yelled, "They're going to Marina hospital" as I ran and breathed for him, and pressed his chest. I watched his little arms just flopping lifelessly. He was cold and limp, and dead.

We were on the way in less than a minute. Jack was ventilating with the Ambu-bag while Carlos did chest compressions. It was quiet, not like the CPR classes I teach; one, two, three, four, five, six, seven, eight, nine, ten, eleven, twelve, thirteen, fourteen, fifteen, breathe twice; one, two, three... we had done this too often. It wasn't much like a movie this time, too quiet.

"Can you get a line?" Jack asked.

"We're right around the corner" I said. I had just finished a quick radio report to the hospital. "Negative Brotman, he's in asystole, we're in the driveway at Marina now, 63's clear."

We stood there for a while next to the door of the little room he was in, hoping I guess, that they could do something. He was so pale. His lips were so blue.

I didn't even remember seeing the police while we were there. I found out later they had arrived just before we did. They didn't know what to do; they had just stood there. A female officer was in a chair in the hallway, she was crying. Her partner was a big guy, he always seemed so big and nasty it made me glad I wasn't a criminal. His eyes gave it away; he wasn't so tough after all.

The firemen were waiting outside the room where Tommy was, taking turns at the tiny window in the door. In the room it was very serious. Nobody was joking, the way Doctors and Nurses and Paramedics often do. The harsh jokes are a way to relieve the tension and somehow make it less tragic, less real. I could hear the thump of the defibrillator as I looked in. Tommy was naked, he had an IV going, he was intubated, and they were giving him another dose of Epinephrine. He had a slight rhythm on the scope, it was slow and weak and they couldn't feel any pulses with it. I slipped into the room and went over to him and I lifted up his eyelids, his pupils were dilated and non-reactive. The Doctor noticed me looking; he said, "Probably brain dead."

"Yeah" I said, agreeing. I felt a little sick, maybe it was because my little girl was Tommy's age, and maybe it was the family crying in the waiting room.

I went down the hall to the back room to finish my paperwork.

I could hear Tommy's Father and Mother as I walked, "Why did you leave him alone?"

"I was only on the phone for a minute, he was in the house" she cried.

They were both crying as they argued. I closed my eyes. I didn't want to cry…

I could see him; he was so big. He stood there talking and smiling all bundled up. It was so wonderful to be so big, to talk to the ducks and have them talk back, and to have such a nice new red jacket. Life was just great!

Chapter Two
Doesn't bother us...

Paramedic, the word creates pictures. Pictures mostly from T.V. and mostly melodramatic, but not bigger than life, unfortunately, not bigger than life...

It was a summer afternoon in Wilmington. I was working at fire station 38. 38's is a *garden spot*, one of the slower assignments. It's a place where the Firemen go to retire and the Paramedics hope they can last long enough to get to someday.

I was up to my elbows in grease. I had been driving in a different car each shift, this was the third shift and the tune-up on my 'fleet' of battered VW's was almost complete. I could do this here, chances were we wouldn't get a call. Well that was the plan.

"Rescue 38, respond to a shooting, engine 53 is also responding, reported as an accidental shooting. 16443 Pacific Coast Highway, at the 'High-Top' liquor store, time out 1056, incident number 204, OCD clear."

I was still toweling off the degreaser as we turned onto PCH. We saw the police car up ahead.

As we pulled into the driveway I saw a police officer standing at the side door to the liquor store. A boy about 15 or 16 years old was standing next to him, the boy was crying and shaking his head.

"What have you got?" I asked as I approached the officer.

"Looks like an accidental, with a shotgun, it's a DB."

Often late at night when you're tired a DB is a 'good' call. If it's a *dead body,* then you can get the paperwork done quick and get back to sleep. But this wasn't a 'good' DB. This was the best friend of the boy at the side door. The boy on the floor was 16 years old. He and his friend were working with an older brother at the family liquor store. The two younger boys were sent to the back room to bring the shotgun up front. They stored it in the locked back room and moved it up front, under the counter, during business hours. It was just one of those things, those freak accidents. The gun had a round in the chamber. Somehow the trigger was bumped as the gun was taken off the rack. In a horrible instant, the 12 gauge double 00 buckshot was discharged. What are the chances? I mean for the accident to happen at all, for the safety to be off, for a round to be chambered, to bump the trigger just right, and for the barrel to just happen to be pointing at the boy's face, from 3 feet away, what are the odds?... couldn't happen, *shouldn't* happen. I imagine his parents often have that thought, why "their" son, how?

We examined him, pronounced him dead, filled out the form, and headed back toward the station.

My partner turned to me, "That was pretty nasty."
"Yea, imagine how his friend feels" I added.

Of course neither of us could imagine it. I get a better idea now, years later. I still feel it, *some* of the grief, *some* of the pain. Just being close to so much tragedy, you absorb it, it permeates you. Somewhere deep inside, somewhere we hope it's swallowed up. We cover it over with a sick joke, we dismiss it, we forget it. We're so callused, so cold. Doesn't bother us...

Chapter Three
Porky Pig

Paramedics have a good time; we have to.

You develop a routine, not just habits or the regular way you approach the job, I mean a 'routine.' Your monologue, a handful of stolen jokes for that week. You work on new impressions or cartoon characters or practice *Elvis* or *John Wayne*. Now I know other Paramedics will read this and say there are a handful of wanna-be comedians who are temporarily Paramedics, but to say Paramedics as a group are like that, no way.

I tried a little experiment. I worked with a guy I had known for a couple of years, who is not particularly loud or outspoken, and come to think of it, I had never heard him tell a joke. So I figured I'd test my assumption.

I had scarcely gotten half way into my best *Elmer Fudd* when he blurted out a top-notch *Sylvester*, followed it with a *Tweety-bird*, and capped it off with a *Yogi bear* and a *Boo-boo*. We spent the rest of the shift performing to each other and to any other Paramedics who would listen. My theory is correct. I know that any Paramedic who says otherwise, secretly, in the confines of his car, on the way to work, when no one else can hear, launches into an impromptu *Jimmy Stewart* or sneaks in a *Porky Pig*.

Chapter Four
"Does he need stitches?"

When someone finds out you're a Paramedic a couple of things *always* occur. The first thing you usually hear goes something like this, "You must see a lot of gruesome things." "How can you stand all the blood?" "Have you ever seen a dead person?"

You get the picture. The second most common response is to relay to you their family's medical history. "Yea my dad had a heart attack and the Paramedics saved him" or "Last year my cousin fell off a ladder and broke his leg" etc., etc.

Probably the worst thing is when, involuntarily, you become a neighborhood urgent care facility when you're off duty. "Sorry to bother you but Johnny fell out of his high chair." Johnny is thrust screaming and bloody into your arms. "Does he need stitches? He's acting sleepy, should I let him go to sleep?" etc., etc. Personally, I have a lot of difficulty telling a neighbor *not* to take Johnny to the doctor or "No, he doesn't need stitches." God forbid Johnny should have a scar when his cut heals, and guess whose fault it is?

Enough said. When Johnny falls down you'll do it anyway, and you know what? It's O.K. We expect it.

Chapter Five
Blood and guts

You know the saying, "Your imagination is always worse than reality." It's not.

Paramedics are regularly exposed to *horrendous* sights. The ones that you 'can' imagine give you a good reference to start with.

After a particularly difficult call my partner began to show some signs of what has become known in the business as "critical incident stress" or more recently "post-traumatic stress disorder." I'll talk later about that particular call, but what occurred to me while he was undergoing 'stress debriefing' was a revelation. The realization that there were probably *dozens and dozens* of calls which have left a significant impact on me and probably on *every* Paramedic; the sights and sounds and smells which we will forever carry in our memories.

I began to list the calls that I could remember vividly. The unique or particularly gruesome, the disgusting, calls which left behind a picture. I quickly listed 50 such mental pictures and decided to stop.

Words cannot adequately relay the impact of these scenes, thank God they can't. Each call is made up of many factors that affect one's response to it, and the ultimate impact from it; the time of day, the added drama of darkness or the vivid colors of day. The type of weather, the sound of the bystanders, the gasps of horror from the crowd as you expose an open fracture or an amputation. The screams of pain and the smells; of burned or rotting flesh, of urine, feces, and vomit; the sight of someone's life's blood filling a gutter, pieces of bones, limbs and digits, the whispers of the dying, the sound of a person's last breath, the feel of a cold stiff body, the look of death.

The pictures I *can* describe lack that three-dimensional quality. The impact of these scenes is uniquely human, and strictly personal. It goes deep and doesn't leave us. We hope to keep them there, down deep, but they're there.

Chapter Six
The reality business

The news strives to capture the horrible, the realities of life, all the things we pray never happen to us. In the news business, "If it bleeds it leads."

These images; they condense and colorize them, then slap us with them daily. We become numbed to it. At home in our living rooms we can view the body of a murdered child then pass the potatoes. We see it in color, the soldier crumpled in the street bloodied and broken, as we load the dishwasher.

Our children, they see it too, too much too soon and too young.

It must seem unreal to most who casually watch the news and see the day's horrors, these pictures without that *third dimension*.

To me that other dimension is there, it comes through the speaker in my car and through the TV screen. The familiar wails of a mother's disbelief fill my ears; I've walked through the blood. I've picked up the bodies. I've held their hands.

Sometimes, when I listen to the radio or TV news, even the *tears* come through, and trickle coldly down my cheek.

Chapter Seven
Impact

The overwhelming impact of the Job is negative; recollections on a career will reflect this.

Think about it, how often does someone call 9-1-1 to say *"Everything is going great! We're all having a very pleasant day. Everyone is healthy, our family is together, and we have a new PUPPY named Tiger. Could you please send the Paramedics out here, we would like to give them some cookies we baked today."* Doesn't happen, does it. For EMT's and Paramedics, most often it's human suffering and tragedy that calls us out.

Of course it's not *all* negative. The rewards can be direct and immediate, like delivering a healthy baby and watching a new mother's glow as you place her newborn child in her arms, or finding out that the 'full arrest' you brought in two hours ago is awake in the ICU. A person was *dead* when you got there, and you brought them back. Now that's a nice feeling... that's a *great* feeling.

Helping people, making a difference in their life, that's what it's all about. One of those positive calls can help dissolve a hundred nightmares.

Chapter Eight
By their dying

Suicide. *Sometimes* you understand it. The old man with cancer, in pain for years, with no hope of recovery; dead really, but doomed to live and suffer, to waste away; a helpless object at the end, no longer a man. We can see the thinking there. Maybe it's wrong, we may disagree with it, but we have a grasp of it.

The hopelessness is what pervades the event. They felt *this* was the only way out. The solution was to no longer *be*. A non-solution really, no drive left to 'tough it out', no hope. The family and friends are left to forever wonder what *might have been,* if they had only seen it coming. They "should have done something." The guilt is often overwhelming for those who are left behind. What might have been, if only they had done this or that differently?

I'm often hit by the selfishness of the act, how they could do this *to* the people they love. Too many times it's the family that find them, and that terrible vision is forever burned in their hearts. Often it's just too hard to live in the house where this happened, the vision is too intense there. How could they do that to the people they love?

I've read the notes. The suicidal person often thinks they will relieve friends or family of a tremendous burden by their dying. If only the person contemplating suicide could read the note that the *family might write,* after they're gone... if they knew *this* would it have made a difference?

Dear Son/Daughter/Mother/Father;

We miss you. Oh how we loved you, but somehow I guess we never let you know how much. You couldn't have known how much we cared about you and have done this.

If only you were here again, I would hold you and tell you how much you mean to me, how I'm here for you if you need me. You can come to me, you are a part of me; when you hurt so do I, when you feel there is no nope, I'll remind you that I need you in my life.

Be strong and realize better days <u>will</u> come, and I want to share them with you. I do love you and you mean so very much to me. A part of me has died and I miss you so much.

Chapter Nine
Her straw hat

She was 16. Problems with her boyfriend is all I could find out. Her dad opened the garage and there she was, his little girl.

She used to love to play horsey when she was three, his little Princess up on his back. "Giddy-up Daddy." Her little straw hat was too big, it kept falling off.

She was hanging there, an extension cord around her neck. She'd been dead for a couple of hours, he could tell. She was so blue. Her eyes were wide open, just staring, no life in them. Her tongue protruded a little between her cold blue lips. He couldn't do anything; it was over.

He called 9-1-1 then gathered the littler kids.

I don't know what he told them, how could he explain it to them. I told him I would need to ask him a few questions. He sat down. "OK" he said. He didn't cry but his eyes were full of pain. He didn't look at me; he looked toward the wall.

It was a black and white picture, a younger him, his little girl on his back, such big smiles; and the straw hat, frozen in mid-air.

Chapter Ten
...and then I cried.

I've never cried during a call. A couple of times I've come close...

I can take a deep breath and push it aside, I think you have to. You deal with so much tragedy, there's a *reason* to cry every day, but you can't. You wouldn't last long in this job if you allowed it to get to you, if you took it personally. So it gets pushed aside. It's been *many* years for me; I've pushed a lot aside and have never really felt the worse for it, I can handle it. I've become callused to it I guess.

Delayed stress response they would call it. All the years, all the tears not shed, finally catching up to you. I can see it in some of my fellow Paramedics, their attitude becomes bitter, they complain a lot more. Some of the honest ones tell me the job bothers them now. Some of them are "Burned-out." That term is too real for many; for Doctors, Nurses, EMT's, Paramedics; the images are burned into us, the stresses become too much, their "Bedside manner" becomes blunt and rough. They should quit, but they don't, they continue but they've had too much.

For me these written reflections on the past are the hardest, it brings them to the surface. The ghosts become real again.

Lately, I find myself touched by the pain around me; it comes to me mostly away from the job listening to the radio on the way to work, and writing down these memories. Sometimes it hits me, some distant event, some tragedy somewhere, a glimpse of pain through the T.V., and suddenly

I just can't push it away, I can *feel* their pain.

It's there; all the years and tears not cried, like a thousand stones collected one by one, and finally the pockets are full. I pushed it aside and pushed it aside, all these years, and then I cried.

Chapter Eleven

"I'm stuck to it"

"Rescue 13, respond to a *sick*, at the Alvarado Hotel. 1037 W. 6th Street, Time 1129, Incident number 243, OCD clear."

13's is a busy spot, I was not happy there. The guys were great and I did have some good times, but it was just *too* busy.

We start at 6:30 a.m. and work until 6:30 the next morning. Sometimes you could watch the Sun come up, and set, and come up again, and never get a chance to make up your bed. I had the feeling this was one of those days. 11:30 in the morning and seven runs already.

We turned on Sixth Street and pulled up in front of the address. We knew the place, a rundown hotel full of roaches and derelicts. An old man at the front door waved to us. My partner grabbed the 'white box,' which contained bandages and a blood pressure cuff. We saw the patient waving to us in the lobby so we decided not to take in the 'big box' with the IVs and medications in it. Seemed like a BS call so far.

The man was sitting in a wheel chair, smiling. "What's wrong today?" I asked.

"Can't get out-a ma chair" he said, with a big toothless grin.

"What do you mean you can't get out of your chair, are you weak? Can you normally get up from your chair?"

"I'm stuck to it." His smile showed a little distress now. His trousers were down around his knees and a dirty blanket covered his lap.

"When was the last time you were out of your chair?"

"Bout three days ago," he said. I looked at my partner, he looked at me, and we sighed in unison.

This man was dirty. He smelled like you might expect him to smell after three days sitting in that chair. I bent down to get a look and asked him to try to stand up slowly. He pushed with both hands on the arm rests, and his butt moved up a half an inch. I heard an awful, wet, squishing sound and was hit with a wave of putrid odor.

There beneath him were hundreds of pulsating *maggots*. They had neatly removed the rotten flesh and were squirming around in a deep, bright red cavity which covered about ten inches of surface, and extended at least two inches deep into his right buttock. Dozens of the little rascals spilled out and fell to the ground. I felt a little sick. Not necessarily at the sight, but at the prospect of sitting in the back of the ambulance with this man during the ride to the hospital.

We poured an antiseptic solution over the area to flush out the maggots, then carefully helped him out of the wheel chair; being careful not to pull off any more skin that was stuck there.

Well, there is more, about how the maggots crawled up and into my boot and the jokes my partner made at dinner that evening about the rice, but I'm getting a little ill so...

Chapter Twelve
Every Twenty Minutes

Sometimes life just doesn't allow mistakes.

She thought the cars had stopped, so with her grandson by one hand and her granddaughter by the other, she began to cross the street. Two cars had stopped, but the one in the 'gutter lane' just kept coming.

I imagine he never did see them, he was driving too fast, he was too drunk, and grandma was too trusting. They were all killed, grandma and the two kids. Not the driver though, he was O.K. It happens too often like that, the drunk driver doesn't get killed, he just kills.

It's hard as a Paramedic, to pronounce the *victims* dead, to put a sheet over a crushed and mutilated child, and then to bandage the cut forehead of the drunk driver. There is something primal there, a call for retribution.

It would be easier if you could trust in the judicial system to appropriately punish the offender. But, more often than not he gets off, he repeats his crime, he drinks and drives again. Society shakes its collective head in disgust, and the cycle continues. We need to blame the courts, and the laws that allow them to do it again and again.

* Each year 26,000 American men, women and children die, and another 1.5 million are injured by drunk drivers.

* The annual costs in lost wages, medical and legal expenses, productivity, etc., caused by drunk driving

accidents is more than $24 billion dollars.

* Drunk drivers are killing 70 people each and every day...or one person every 20 minutes.

Statistics, posters, T. V. commercials, newspaper ads and pamphlets; you know what they lack? They don't relay the urgency, they haven't *put* you there. If you saw the little stuffed bear lying in the street, and had to step over the insides of a little girl to pronounce her dead, if people saw the horrible, real, and daily reality of it, maybe, maybe, things would change. Maybe the *victim* would become the most important person in the tragedy, and maybe it would be harder to muster compassion for the drunk driver. I have *no* compassion for them. I've looked into the lifeless eyes of too many victims.

* Those statistics are old, I imagine it is much worse now, I don't want to check.

Chapter Thirteen
Venice

It was a nice day. We had just finished our ritual drive along Ocean Front Walk in Venice.

It's a pedestrian walkway, of course roller skating is allowed too, it is Venice Beach. Bicyclists have a separate path and are fined for riding on the "boardwalk."

The Police ride bikes here, and wear shorts and blue polo shirts, and have guns. This is a strange place.

Venice. It's a community made up of either 60's kids grown up or 90's kids dying to be 60's kids, and of course the kids who are just trying to 'be.' Then there's the homeless, of all sorts, and shapes, colors, and smells. And there's the retired folks, and the yuppies with those million-dollar beach houses, and the required BMW, Mercedes, Jaguar or Rolls in the driveway; I think it's an ordinance. Let's see, who's *not* here in Venice? Oh yeah, the "normal" people don't live here, they just visit. Boy do they visit! Every summer day the 'walk' is a mass of, well, excuse the generalization, *humanity*. They come here to *watch*. They watch the Venice locals put on their shows. There's a guy who juggles chain saws, yes they're real and they're running! There's the acrobats and mimes, the rappers, the break dancers, the skaters, the guitar playing turban-headed singing roller-skater, and the sellers; of jewelry, hats, shoes, T-shirts, quartz crystals, African carvings, Mexican blankets, leather dresses, paintings, ice cream, pizza (deep breath); and the petitions: to save the whales, save the beach, save the pup fish and Mono lake, and to save the trees, and Earth, and save Venice Beach, and stop nuclear power, and of course to make marijuana legal (which eventually worked!.) It's a funny place. I didn't mention the girls.

Ahhh. Life is wonderful, sometimes...

"Rescue 63."
"63 go."
"Rescue 63, a person down at 10263 Washington Blvd., time out 1135, incident 98, OCD clear."

We didn't turn on our siren, not in that crowd, two things would have happened. A third of the crowd would have jumped, startled, out of the way, colliding into the people next to them and either hurt themselves or somebody else or piss-off someone and end up getting thumped. The other two-thirds of the crowd would have continued on their way as if nothing had changed, and would occasionally look over their shoulder to give us a dirty look, for daring to think that anything could be more important than their stroll along the boardwalk, and their enjoyment of their melting *'Dove bars.'* It just wasn't worth the frustration for any of us.

We put on our flashing lights, and *lightly* tapped our horn, ever so politely, it barely had a chance to actually 'beep' it just *clicked.*

A gentle ripple of movement flowed through the crowd and the sea slowly parted in front of us. In physics this is known as the *Charleton Heston* effect.

We were just down the street from the address, it was the *'New York Pizza'* place. I could see people inside backing away from a man as we pulled up.

The manager was inside. He looked out at us, then pointed toward the man just outside his doorway. The man, about 20, just stood there. There was an outside dining area with four or five little round tables and two chairs around each one. We were still in the ambulance. I motioned to one of the bystanders and he came up to my window.

"What's going on here"? I asked.

"This guy is wacko. He started screaming and knocked over a table. He tried to burn a kid with a cigarette. He's on something."

"O.K. Thanks."

The crazy guy looked at us then looked at one of the kids who had moved about 10 feet away from him, to a corner near a table. The crazy guy looked back toward me, then began walking slowly toward the youngster, who was trapped in the corner. My partner was already on the radio calling for the P.D. I quickly got out of the ambulance and headed toward the man.

"Hey, come over here" I said gently. "I need to talk to you." The man stopped where he was, he was only five feet from the boy. "Somebody called us because they thought you might need some help, are you O.K.?"

He smiled and said, "I'm O.K."

"Can you come over here, I need to ask you some questions and take your blood pressure, all right?" He stood where he was looking a little bit like Jack Nicholson in one of his semi-crazy scenes from *The Shining*. My partner was close by, he motioned the other people out of the way. "So what's your name?" I asked.

"Who cares" he said.

"Let me take your pulse, if everything is all right we can get out of here." I was afraid he was going to hurt the boy, who stood wide-eyed and frozen in the corner. I wanted to get close enough to control this guy. *(Where's a cop when you need one).* I inched forward slowly. "Somebody called 9-1-1 because they were worried about you. Are you all right?"

"Take my pulse, you can tell I'm all right" he said with that Nicholson smile.

"O.K., we just want to make sure you're O.K. My name is Lance, I'm a Paramedic. Do you take any medicines for anything?" I was next to him now.

"No." The Nicholson smile was gone.

I had my left hand on his wrist and my right hand under

his elbow. I *was* checking his pulse but that wasn't my concern at the moment. I wanted to be able to control him if I needed to. My left foot was slightly forward, my right foot slightly back. My left side was facing him. (Looks like trouble doesn't it?) Well it was, he looked in my eyes, and the Nicholson smile came back, the one where Jack takes an axe and breaks through a door; he glanced down at the chair in front of him. His right hand jerked toward the chair. His fingers were about six inches from the chair when the line which divides harmless craziness from a real threat was crossed. I pushed up on his elbow locking his arm, shoved him backward into a brick wall, and then quickly forward off balance onto his face. Blood came from his nose as he smashed into the concrete. He went limp, "I'm sorry" he said.

My knee was in his back, his left arm was twisted behind him. My partner was holding his right arm in a similar lock in the small of the man's back. "I'm sorry" he said again.

"Just hold still, don't move an inch or I'll twist your arm off."

I gave it a little turn. "O.K., O.K!"

Well the Police showed up, they handcuffed him, and took him in the Police car to the emergency room. I found out later the guy was a *little* crazy; no kidding. Life in Venice.

I've always thought if a Paramedic is ever killed in L.A. it would be in Bel Air or Pacific Palisades, or Venice; someplace you don't *expect* it. It's a dangerous job, you just never know.

Chapter Fourteen

"60 Minutes"

The Los Angeles City Fire Department changed its dispatching system a while back, finally. The Paramedics had been warning the department for years that the way they were dispatching was dangerous.

They were killing people. We told everybody but no one seemed to care. I think it was when *60 Minutes* told them that it finally hit home.

"60 Minutes" was in town, somebody was dead, and the F.D. had a lot of explaining to do. The Fire Department battened up the hatches and stayed unavailable for comment. What else could they do? It was true, all of it, the system was lousy, people were being killed, and they were in deep trouble, multi-million-dollar trouble.

If you had asked them back then to tell you what a dispatcher asked a caller, or how they decided what equipment to send out, or how would they help a mother revive her drowned child while waiting for the ambulance to arrive, well, you would have gotten a dozen different answers, depending on who you asked. The system was a "seat-of-the-pants" affair, based largely on "gut feelings." That was 1988. A lifetime ago.

The dispatch system in place now is state-of-the-art. People are not killed by it, they're helped. In L.A. a call to 9-1-1 will have appropriate resources dispatched rapidly, and the caller is given *pre-arrival instructions* over the phone, to guide them through first-aid procedures until help arrives. Finally.

What is so hard to take about this whole dispatch business, and the bureaucracy of a big city, is that they *knew*. It wasn't a bureaucracy moving slowly, it was a bureaucracy at a dead stop. It was management's unwillingness to move forward. Leadership that had lost sight of its purpose; to save lives, to help people, to *really* care, not to just say it, but to 'feel' it.

Chapter Fifteen
Trained buttons

A patient's medical information is confidential. A Paramedic is like a doctor in that regard.

Whatever personal information a Paramedic obtains remains *strictly* confidential. Of course we do tell the Doctor, and the Nurses, and our partners, and any other Paramedic we work with, and of course our wives, and their friends, and anyone we know who will listen, and of course strangers who we happen to meet and talk to. But, other than that, it is *strictly* confidential, for our ears only. Seriously, we can't share the 'specifics' such as 'Who' the patient was, that's confidential. But I assume there's some *statute of limitations*, maybe thirty years I hope; I'm not sure.

A famous heavy weight boxer, who fought Mohammed Ali, was driving home from a social function and crashed his white *Excalibur*. His car went off the freeway, over the embankment and crashed into a tree.

We got the call as a T/A (traffic accident), at 2 a.m. We got to the reported location but couldn't find a thing. "Turn right" I said. We took a street which paralleled the freeway. "Over there!" A man was crawling on all fours, up the embankment toward the freeway. "OCD Rescue 13."

"13 go."

"OCD 13, send us an engine for manpower, just east of Vermont on 12th street, notify the engine we'll be up on the freeway embankment at that location."

"13 roger, you'll be getting your engine."

"Roger."

We hopped the chain link fence and headed over to the man.

"I'll check the car" shouted my partner.

"O.K." I headed toward the man. He was *big*. He was wearing a tuxedo. He kept crawling up the incline looking from side to side, half moaning and half mumbling, it was dark.

"Sir!" I shouted. "It's the Paramedics, hold still I want to help you." He flopped over to his side, then just rolled over on his back, with his arms straight out like a giant cross. I continued to talk to him as I moved closer. "Don't move, you've been in a car accident, we're going to help you."

He sat bolt upright, eyes wide, fists clenched. He had a laceration on his lip, a deep one, it would need stitches. "It's the Paramedics, don't move, you're hurt, you've been in a car accident." He starred at me, his fists were still clenched. I shined my flashlight across his body. His pants were torn and I saw blood on his leg. That face... I knew him from somewhere.

My partner had checked the car and was heading over to me. "Nobody in the car" he said.

"Check around in those bushes in case someone was thrown out." I pointed to the large bushes surrounding the car. "And we'll need C-spine stuff for this guy when the Engine gets here, he's pretty confused."

"The steering wheel is intact" my partner reported, "And the windshield isn't broken, but there's some blood on the top of the steering wheel and on the driver's side floor."

"O.K" I said. "Where do you hurt?" I asked the man.

"What happened?" he asked in a daze. I knew him now.

"You were in a car accident. Don't move around, you're hurt. Just hold still we're going to take you to the hospital."

"What?" he said, with a puzzled look.

"We're the Paramedics..." His right hand raised slightly, I got the impression he was trying to decide whether to give me a right cross or just a quick jab. I kept a safe distance. I knew we would need some help, this guy was built like a tank. I heard the rumble of the engine company as they turned the corner.

The plan would be to stabilize the patient's neck with a cervical collar and then place him on a long backboard. The backboard would keep his spinal column in line and help prevent further injury or paralysis if he had damaged his spine. I didn't really think there was much chance of that, after all he had just went through a complete range of motion of his neck and back while climbing around the embankment. But it was protocol, and better safe than... you know. The Engine Captain came up to me and asked, "What have you got?" I described the man's injuries and told him who he was.

"You know, the boxer" I said.

"Yeah that is him!" he said.

"We'll need all the C-spine stuff and a flat stretcher." I called out to a Fireman nearby.

"You want the gurney set up by the fence?"

"Yeah, that'll be good. Hey Cap would you call OCD and request EMS out here (that meant the EMS *Supervisor*) the press will probably get notified" I said.

Up the embankment my partner and the Firemen were trying to convince the patient we were there to help, and that he needed to do what we asked him to do. He would only say "What happened?"

"That's the fourth time he's asked" my partner reminded me. That was bad. *Repetitive questioning* is one of the signs of a head injury. I wanted to get him going.

"Look. ..." I called him by his first name. "We need to lay you down on this board to keep your back straight, and get you to the hospital so they can check you out." He raised his clinched fist and stared at me blankly. I took a flashlight and shined it up at the Fireman. I hoped the fire helmet would convince him it was all right. "See, it's the Fire Department, we're going to help you." He laid back, and the board was placed at his side. We explained every step as we rolled him onto his side then back on the board.

I tried to tear his shirt open to examine his chest. I was used to cheap shirts, the kind I wear; the shirts whose buttons fall off during *normal use*, and are launched simultaneously into orbit by grabbing the shirt and pulling. But *these* buttons were a different species. These buttons knew their purpose in life, and seemed to hold on *tighter* as I pulled. What I had run into here was a very expensive silk shirt, with *trained buttons*. Awesome. I didn't want to spend too much time within striking range, and the shirt was already torn, so out came my trusty rescue scissors and off went the shirt and bow-tie. I cut the trousers up to expose both legs. He had some nasty cuts to both knees. We packaged him up, and with six of us on the stretcher, carried him to the gurney. He seemed to improve rapidly and was joking as we rolled into the E.R. He was O.K., still a little dingy, but O.K.

He gave me his home phone number and asked me to call his wife. It was 2:35 a.m. I woke her up and let her know her husband was O.K., and that he was at *California Hospital*.

He said later that someone on the freeway had cut him off and forced his car off the road. He got some stitches and did all right. No it's not Spinks.

L.A. City Paramedics have treated some very famous folks. I seem to have missed the limelight though. Oh yeah, I did take *Mrs. Olson*, the *Folger* coffee lady, to the hospital. She's was a very nice lady. (The accent is fake though) and those Folger coffee commercials haven't been on TV since TV's still had antennas, so of course only 'old people' remember her. She may have been the lady who was the Wicked Witch of the East, or West, in the *Wizard of Oz*, is that possible? No. Well she *looked* like her. I'll have to *Google* that. I don't think it could have been her, she wasn't *that* old. And I bandaged the hand of some girl from the *Brady Bunch*, who got a little cut while loading her dishwasher. I'll change her name to hide her identity, *Martha*. She was mad because I didn't think her little cut was too impressive, and I wouldn't take her to the hospital in the Paramedic ambulance.

I've met *Martha Ray*, who? And took her relative to the hospital. She seemed like a pleasant person who was *old* <u>then</u>; she was more of my *parent's* generation. She was an actress/comedian who was famous for her big mouth. I *almost* treated *Ronald Mc Donald*, but the stagehand got bopped in the head instead of Ronald, darn it. I probably could have gotten some free fries out of that one.

Oh there's a few more, but I'm good at keeping secrets.

Chapter Sixteen
I remember now

The call was for an *attempted suicide.*

That's usually a 'nothing' call; a distraught teenager who took four *Excedrin* because her mother grounded her for coming home after 11:00, or the little boy who *may* have eaten rat poison. Mom says, "Well he was sitting near it." These people usually end up in the hospital, just in case. The concern over liability is so great that more and more we are being forced to take just about everybody to the emergency room, whether they need it or not. And they wonder why the hospitals are overcrowded and going broke.

"OCD, Rescue 53, what is the method of this suicide?" I asked. Not that a person who has, say, overdosed on pills is particularly safe, but an attempted suicide with a butcher knife or a gun is a pretty good tip off that you want to wait for the police before going in.

"Rescue 53 from OCD, no further information, one call from the PD."

"Roger OCD, we're going to hold back until the PD arrive."

"53 Roger" the dispatcher responded back.

"Let's wait right here" I pointed to a spot along the curb, just around the corner from the address and out of view. My partner turned right instead, *then* pulled over.

"Opps" he said, "I thought the address was further down." We had parked two doors from the location.

As we pulled over we could see a lady standing on the front lawn up ahead; she started waving to us. She was motioning toward the back of the house. We pulled forward and stopped in front of the house next door. I motioned her to come to us. She waved again and started up a pathway toward the backyard. I called to her from the ambulance, "Come over here, I need to talk to you first!"

I try not to walk into an incident without a pretty good idea of what is going on, especially an attempted suicide. We don't just follow people into the great unknown.

"He's back here" she said, and started walking away. I stepped out of the ambulance and walked toward her. "Wait, come over here!" I was more demanding now. "What happened back there?"

"He's been upset. He wants to kill himself. He's back here in the bathroom. I'll show you."

I reached out and took her by her shoulder. "Does he have any weapons in the house?"

"He has a gun and said he'll kill anybody who comes near him."

"Well in that case we're not going back there until the police get here. You stay here with us." A black and white arrived about then. I told him what we had and the Sergeant called for the S.W.A.T team. Within about 45 minutes SWAT had arrived. After a considerable time planning the operation they headed to the back of the house. Several shots followed. Within a few moments, a SWAT member motioned us back to the rear of the house. My partner waited about twenty feet away. If the guy was dead, and I figured he would be, you don't want more people than necessary tromping around a crime scene disturbing evidence.

He was slumped there in the corner of the bathroom. He had several bullet holes in him, including one "between the eyes." I checked him, made note of visible brain matter, and pronounced him dead. I went back to the Rescue, filled out the paperwork, gave the 'pink copy' to the police and we left.

I'm frequently reminded of the sad state of our judicial system, and the tremendous bureaucratic overload when I receive a subpoena for an incident that happened *years* earlier. On a traffic accident case for instance; in two years the typical L. A. City Paramedic may go on more than 500 traffic accident calls. And we're supposed to remember, under oath, if it was a blue Chevy or if the man was wearing a sweat shirt or a T-shirt. Well, needless to say, there's a lot of "I don't recall" going on if we end up testifying in a case like that. But this call was different. It was *somewhat* unusual, and knowing it would probably result in some sort of legal action, I made sure my Journal entry was detailed. I remember this case well.

Paramedics *like* the police, and generally I think the police *like* the Paramedics. We work in close proximity, we joke with each other at the scene of incidents or at the hospitals, and wave or honk when we drive past each other at work. I feel I'm generally immune from a speeding ticket within L.A. City limits. (Luckily I've never actually tested this theory). I say this about our relationship with the police because I respect the difficult situations they encounter, and believe they are out there doing their best to do a good job. They're out there night after night putting their butts on the line against the worst elements of our society, trying to keep us safe, well, safer. And trying to make sure *they* go home to their families at the end of their shift. I know I wouldn't sleep well at night knowing that I, through some technicality, helped to get a good officer fired, or perhaps land him in jail. What I'm getting at is the stories, in the bathroom shooting, *theirs* vs. mine.

I was subpoenaed to court. I got a call to go up to the DA's office at City Hall the day of the court case. He wanted to talk with me before the hearing.

I was guided down a maze of skinny corridors with boxes of documents piled along the walls, and finally reached his office. As I opened the door a man in a suit had a 38-caliber pistol pointed at me. The man in the suit was a police officer, he had the gun in his right hand across his chest. He told the attorney across the desk, "It was right here like this when it went off. That explains the bullet in the wall and the powder burns. It was pushed into that angle during the struggle."

The attorney scratched his chin, "O.K. I can see that."

"I'm the Paramedic who was on the call, do you want me to wait outside?"

"No, no, have a seat, we're just going over some things before going to court. The prosecution is saying he couldn't have fired the shot into the wall."

The officer went on to demonstrate again, "Like this, kind of over his shoulder."

"O.K. we can explain that" the Attorney said, nodding his head. "We're just trying to explain the placement of a bullet in the bathroom wall" he said to me. "What we need you to do is testify to the times you recorded on your form. The family says it was over 40 minutes before the police allowed you guys back to the body."

"No not at all" I said. "They called us right back there after the shots. It was probably forty minutes or more from the time we arrived, but right away after the shots."

"Good" said the DA. "Your form shows just a couple of minutes. So you went back there and pronounced him dead, how many bullet wounds did you see?"

"Well he was slumped in the corner. He had a number of holes in his chest, and one in the forehead. He had the gun over his chest so..."

"What?" the DA interrupted.

"The gun was in his right hand like this" I demonstrated.

The attorney got a little pale at this point. "It's been over a year since the incident, you're probably not clear on some of the details. Take a minute to think back on it."

"No, I'm sure the gun was in his hand and crossed over his chest like this."

The DA sat down and muttered something like, "This is a real problem." The two officers in the room didn't say a word as the DA said, "The officer's reports state that the gun went off and was taken away from him during a struggle. He wouldn't have had the gun when you were called in, it had been put over near the sink area."

"No, he was holding the gun" I said.

The DA was silent for a *long* 15 seconds, as he stared down at his desk. Nobody else said a thing. "We can't use you then. Let me think about this." He took about a half a minute to stare at the wall and back down at his desk. "I want to remind everyone in this room that everything that has been said here today is attorney/client privilege and cannot be discussed with anyone." The attorney turned to the police officer and said, "We can't use this form at all for the times, it will lead to *him*."

"Him" was me and I could tell by this point, I had put a pretty big fly in the ointment. I didn't have the whole picture, and didn't know why their story would be different than mine, but I felt guilty somehow anyway.

The attorney scratched his head one last time then said. "O.K. Thanks, it's been a long time and sometimes memories get distorted. Thanks for coming."

"That's it?" I said.

"That's all, we won't need you, thank you."

"O.K, good luck" I said, glancing one last time at the SWAT officer who had sat quietly during this exchange; he was looking down, sheepishly.

On the way home from work the next day the local radio news station mentioned the case. It was a big deal. The officers were found not guilty. The family of the dead man had alleged that he was unconscious from a heroin overdose, and was slumped in the corner of the bathroom. And that the SWAT team had just kicked in the door and executed him to "get it over with." The sister of the man said she had seen him in there before they called the Paramedics, and that he was unconscious, with the gun in his hand across his chest.

I've thought of this incident a lot and have mixed emotions about it. The police must keep *their* safety as a prime concern during incidents like these. The man did have a gun. He had threatened to kill anybody who came through the door. Given that, the officers were ready to do what they had to do, to make sure they went home to their families that night.

What if they went in, saw the gun, and in that split second, when they believed they were about to be killed, responded by opening up on the man to protect themselves, and realized too late he had made no move, and in fact may have been unconscious when they fired. What if 'they' pulled the trigger of his gun to better justify what had occurred. Who would know? After I had pronounced the man dead they removed the gun and put it on the sink. Then got together to construct a 'better' scenario than the real life one. So what, they were doing their job, the man did appear to pose a deadly threat when they fired, he did have a gun. The decision to shoot or not when they entered that room had to be made in an instant. No one would know, it would be so much cleaner this way. They did what they felt was best for all concerned, they didn't really do anything wrong, so why not?

Interesting story. You know, the more I think about it now the more I realize the attorney was right. It was a long time ago, and your memory can play tricks on you. I guess he wasn't holding the gun after all. No, it was over by the sink, that's right, I remember now.

Chapter Seventeen
Cookies and Cantaloupes

People frequently ask "What's the worst thing you've ever seen?"

It's a hard question for me to answer. In this job it's a common occurrence to see and deal directly with scenes of such brutality, and injuries so horrendous, that sometimes they defy description. I don't dwell on these images. I try to forget them.

It figured, the lady had just handed us the bag with our *Egg Mc Muffins*. The call was to an auto junk yard. There was an old rusted 50-gallon drum being used as a fireplace, and a dead man in a kneeling position near it. As we came closer we could see his hands were around his abdomen, as if he were trying to hold on to something. There had been some sort of argument I guess, and he lost. The knife had sliced across his abdomen, spilling the majority of his intestines on the ground. Not particularly unusual, and not much work to do, just complete the necessary paperwork and call for the police. The worst part of the call, was the cold Egg McMuffins. My partner and I decided to shop for a 12-volt microwave for the rescue.

It was the first call of the day; an injury on the train track. The Engineer said it looked like the guy jumped in front of the train. It worked. We found an arm as we walked down the track and a large blood spot. The rest was just a jumble. A finger here, an ear and some hair, some organ (maybe a lung) and assorted bone pieces and meat, all mushed up in a lump. An arm doesn't weigh much really, I remember thinking as I carried it over closer to what had been the body. I guess I've watched too many late-night horror films, because I sort of expected the hand to try to strangle me.

I remember one call that gave me the chills, you know, the fingernails on the chalk board effect A guy had crashed his car into a light pole. The hood turned sideways and the sharp corner triangular edge of it, where it had been attached, was driven through the windshield at head level. There was a large crowd surrounding the man, maybe 50 people. It's like that in South Central L.A., there's usually a big crowd.

The bystanders had tried to help and had pulled the guy out of the car (the wrong thing to do) and laid him on the sidewalk. The car was full of *Budweiser* cans and a half dozen of them were scattered on the sidewalk. The man was rolling around when we got there, kind-of scratching at his forehead, over and over again, as if he was trying to remove something. Problem was he was pulling out pieces of exposed brain matter from the wound on his head. I guess if he had lived he'd be forced to go into politics, or maybe he could have become a Fire Chief.

The new seat belt law had just gone into effect. Kids under 40 lbs. had to be restrained in child seats and everybody needed to be wearing seat belts. I liked it, I had always worn my seat belt, and knew from experience that it was a good idea and a good law.

They were heading back from the market, a young father and his daughter, bags full of groceries in the back. His little girl was riding in the rear of the station wagon, next to the groceries. I bet she liked it back there. Nobody else was in the car, just her and her Dad. Dad never wore a seat belt. I'm sure he didn't give it much thought, and it was probably more fun for her, back there with the cookies and the cantaloupes.

The accident wasn't his fault. The other car ran a red light, hit his bumper, and spun his car around. No big deal really, the car would live.

The street was littered, all the cookies had spilled. And the little girl, she had been thrown out with the groceries when the tailgate flew open. There was nothing we could do. A cantaloupe lay next to her head. I couldn't tell about some of the parts, they were mixed up; the insides of the girl's head, and the insides of the cantaloupe.

The police office said the father would be charged under the new seat belt law, the first case in L.A. "Good" I thought to myself. I found out about a month later the charges were dropped. The Father had suffered enough from the ordeal they said, and it was probably true, it was too late and too tragic. He didn't deserve to be made an example of, I guess. He probably bought the cookies for her, and he let her ride in the back where it was more fun. Back there with the cookies and the cantaloupes.

Chapter Eighteen
Clean underwear

The dangers of the job are often unexpected, they can sneak up on you.

Like the call to the L.A. Harbor. A ship was unloading cargo and a worker had fallen, sounded like a broken leg from the description as we arrived.

As we worked our way toward the cargo hold, a crew member warned us to watch our step. We were headed down a skinny ladder to the deck below when both of my feet slipped off the rungs. As I hung there by my hands, thirty feet off the ground, the warning hit home.

"What are these things?" I said, pointing to the dozen or so *huge* black cylinders in the cavernous hold below.

"They're graphite insulators" someone called out.

"Pretty slippery" my partner echoed.

I knew we'd have to hoist the man up through the top of the cargo hold. "There's no way to get him back up these ladders, do you have a *Stokes basket* to lower down?" My voice echoed around the massive iron walls to the men above.

"Yeah, I'll call for it." The man radioed another part of the ship, and within 20 minutes and a dozen slips and falls later, we had him splinted, in the ambulance, and ready to go.

In the ambulance, as I turned the first comer, my foot slipped off the brake and onto the gas pedal, knocking my partner in the back into the opposite wall of the ambulance. "Geez!" my partner said, "Nice driving!"

"Sorry" I apologized. I took off my "graphited" boots and drove the rest of the way to the hospital in my socks.

I looked down at my big toe poking through my sock, and realized Mom was right. I had better make sure I always wear clean underwear, and socks with no holes, you just never know.

Chapter Nineteen
Ahhh, life

There are days when you just can't handle the routine.

You can feel miserable and groan and grumble all day, or you can find way to entertain yourself, it was one of those days.

It started when I passed a Fireman's locker and spotted his shirt hanging on the door knob. I passed by at first, then paused, and walked slowly back to the locker. It was natural, instinctual, as I quickly removed the badge and re-attached it upside down. I began to smile as I walked away. It was going to be a wonderful day.

By noon I had rigged a cup of water to fall out of the refrigerator when the door was opened. I turned off the main hot water valve when three people were taking showers. I put a single square of toilet paper in the toaster to Bar-B-Que the next unsuspecting piece of toast. I also took four little packets of mustard, punched a little hole in each of them and put one under every toilet seat lid. The chain reaction had begun. The Firemen and Paramedics were all blaming each other, and of course everyone was denying it. When someone accused me, I just looked at them sternly and said, "I'm too busy to play games" and walked away. Ahhh, life.

I decided to put an end to my mischief about one o'clock in the afternoon. By then two pairs of boots had been filled with whipped cream, three shirts had been soaked then put in the freezer, one Fireman had been "bucketed" (a water drop from the roof or down the pole hole from the second floor onto the victim's head) and I hadn't done *any* of that. It was a snowball rolling downhill and there was no way to stop it. It would be 6:30 tomorrow morning before we could all escape. Until then it was every man for himself. Luckily, we were busy and out of the station most of the day. We played the role of innocent observers to the immature attics of the Firefighters. It was just one of those days.

Chapter Twenty
Elvis

In Los Angeles, the Paramedic II is the lead Paramedic; these terms change, but that's what it was when I was there.

It's a promotional position that requires a test and an oral interview. He (or she) is ultimately responsible for making the decisions and supervising the driver, the Paramedic I. They both have the same training and certification from the County as Paramedics, but the PII has generally been around longer.

One of the roles of the PII is to do most of the questioning of the patient, and to call the run in on the mobile radio (Biocom) if the patient needs medication, some advanced procedure, or happens to fit into one of the dozens of categories which require a "call in."

The base hospital (base station) is contacted and a specially trained Nurse, M.I.C.N. (Mobile Intensive Care Nurse) answers the radio call, and using predetermined standing orders or consulting the hospital physician, gives the Paramedics orders for the procedure or medication.

Remember those characters from "Emergency?" (If you're old enough) Johnny, Roy, Doctor Bracket, and Dixie the Nurse. Well *forty* years later it still works pretty much like that.

The PI and PII can work out some system where they alternate their responsibilities. The PII may do the radio one shift and the PI might start the IVs, whatever. Some guys like to swap, others like to just stick with the familiar. My partner was like that, he didn't like doing the radio, so I was stuck with it *every* day.

I remember one particular evening I was really sick of doing the radio. I was tired and just not in the mood. I felt my reports were sloppy, and I asked my partner if he would do it the rest of the shift. He didn't want to, great.

We got a call for *Chest pain*. "Another work-up" I mumbled. Another radio run.

My partner started the IV and placed an oxygen mask on the patient, while I gathered the necessary medical history and patient complaints for the report. I flipped the switch on, switched the frequency to 9A, and pushed the button which dialed our base.

"USC" came the voice from the Base Station nurse.

"USC, 15 we'll meet you on 4."

"Roger, Rescue 15, 4 Charlie."

"Roger." I noticed the "*Roger*" I gave was a bit slower than normal, and my voice was a little deeper. Maybe it was exhaustion, maybe it was boredom, but a light came on. Suddenly that voice was a bit like *Elvis*, no, it sounded *a lot* like Elvis!

"USC, Rescue 15 on 4, standing by" no... It *was* Elvis.

So I did the rest of the radio report in the best Elvis voice I've ever done. I couldn't help it, it was a force from somewhere higher than me, I think it may have *been* Elvis.

Chapter Twenty-One
Shemana, Luana, Lasheka

I think the less affluent populations of the city tend to come up with the most interesting names for their children.

I don't mean this in a derogatory sense, and the fact that many of these areas are predominantly black should not construe this observation to be a bigoted or anti-racial comment. I don't mean to offend.

Many of the names have origins in Africa, and many are of Swahili variation, and of course many are just 'made up.' To those of us unfamiliar with African culture and language the names may seem, unusual.

Shemana, Luana, Lasheka... The list is endless. The names that are most interesting to me are the *constructed* names. Names derived from bits and pieces of other names, splitting a name in half and putting the end on the front, or using a common object or term as a name. I recall a girl's name "Ureen" spelled "Urine." Or take for example, another real name I encountered, *Ertrob*. Ert-rob, Robert, get it? Interesting.

I went on a call to a 49-year-old man named "Baby Smith." I pictured his mother as she was gently handed her newborn son. She smiled and gently kissed his cheek. She picked up his tiny hand, and there on his wrist, the little blue band proclaimed boldly "Baby Smith." Her smile grew, "What a wonderful hospital" she thought. "They even gave him a name."

The lady had called 911 because her little boy had shut his finger in the refrigerator door a couple of hours ago. She said it still hurt him when he climbed the tree in the front yard, or did a crab walk race with the neighborhood kids, mostly after the third or fourth race.

We were talking to mom on the front porch, and a bunch of kids were playing football. "Which one is your son?" I said, looking toward the mass of kids now racing toward the garden hose, which was the 20-yard line.

"That's him, the one who just tackled that big kid." "Oar-on-ja-low" she screamed. He looked up then ran over to the porch. He stood there looking up. "Showm yo finga" she said. He obligingly held up the index finger on his left hand, looked at it, put it down, and then held up the thumb on his right hand. After a brief exam of *all* the fingers, and an assortment of digital calisthenics, we proclaimed the finger "No emergency" and advised Mom to take him to her private doctor.

"Leee-mon-ja-low" she screamed to her other boy. My curiosity had peaked, and my unofficial *South Central Los Angeles Name Origination Foundation* study was still underway so I asked.

"Your boys have interesting names, Oar-on-ja-low and Lee-mon-ja-low, what do they mean?"

She began to tell me about when she was in the hospital, after giving birth to her twin boys, and couldn't decide on names. A lady from the hospital had just brought by the birth certificates to fill in the names and to sign. She would be back in 15 minutes. Well, mom was flipping channels on the hospital T.V. when *Bill Cosby* appeared. He was smiling that big goofy Cosby smile and was holding up two boxes. "I just can't decide" he said. He looked left, "Orange Jell-O," he looked to the right, "Or Lemon Jell-O, I love em both." The light went on and so did the names on the birth certificates.

Chapter Twenty-Two
Four more hours

She wore dark lacy panties and a skimpy push up bra under her tight, white Nurse's dress.

She was one of the few attractions at County Hospital; circulating among the drunks and derelicts, a sensual treat for the weary Paramedics. After 24, 48, or even 72 hours on the rescue, she was almost too much to take.

It was about 2 a.m. when she appeared at the back door of the ambulance. My partner, myself, and the crew of Rescue 14 were chit chatting, something about the shortage of surgical gloves...

"I went sailing with Taylor over the weekend" she proclaimed cheerfully to the female Paramedic from 14's.

"Oh that sounds neat, who went?"

"There was Taylor and me and two guys who are friends of Taylor. His friend gives sailing lessons, we took his boat, it was great!"

We just stood there silently while they talked.

"But Scott was a little nervous" she said. "Me alone with three guys."

"I guess so" the female paramedic said.

"He asked if I slept with any of them. I said, *no*. He asked if I gave any of them head. I said, *no*. And he asked if I drank any *Jack Daniels*, he knows Jack Daniels makes me get naked."

I'd heard her talk nasty before, but I was still a bit stunned. I think it was a hormone rush, I began fidgeting a bit.

She continued. "I said well, *no*, I had *Tequila*."

I couldn't take it any longer.

"So you only got *half* naked?" I said.

She smiled, "I was good though because I jumped in on the other side of the boat and they didn't even see me."

They continued to gossip about nakedness and giving head and all the while her black lace panties and bra were becoming more and more obvious to me. I found myself studying the pattern in the lace as it climbed over the curves of her breasts. I think she noticed me staring, she smiled a wicked little smile. That was it, I had to leave. I looked over at my partner and gave him the "Let's go" head twitch.

"See ya later" my partner called out as we exited.

"Bye" I said and gave a quick wave.

As we drove down the ramp my partner looked over at me, panting, with his tongue hanging half way out of his mouth. I sighed a deep sigh, and rubbed my face and eyes. Only four more hours, and the shift would be over.

Chapter Twenty-Three
September 78'

I was working at Rescue 82, at Hollywood Blvd. and Bronson. A big chunk of the Hollywood Hills was in our area, including the "Hollywood sign."

I was working with Pat, an "Old timer." He'd been on the job about six years longer than me; I'd been on about a year. He had dozens of stories about the *good old days*, lots of tall tales.

It was a warm summer night, and unknown to us we were about to add another story to our Tall tale's files.

A "Sick" call on Laurel Drive; we rang the bell and waited. The apartment door opened quickly to a young brunette with curly shoulder length hair. "She's in the living room." She turned and led the way. "She's my roommate, she's been vomiting, she's really sick."

We walked in casually. I immediately noticed several large photographs on the wall, a pretty girl modeling various tiny swim suits, and a large photograph in a thick yellow frame of the same girl in a bright yellow skirt and a long sleeve, *unbuttoned*, white blouse, with nothing underneath. It was the brunette.

Her friend was sitting on the couch, her head laid back, staring at the ceiling. "What's bothering you tonight?" I asked as I knelt on one knee next to her.

"I just feel nauseated. I took a *Tums* and it helped a little."

I asked the standard barrage of questions about her medical history, medications, the possibility of pregnancy, unusual bleeding, what and when she ate last, etc., etc. The only significant information I could gather was that she and her friend had been downing wine coolers all night, and were both a bit *blitzed.*

Pat advised her to see a Doctor as I stood to leave. The brunette who had been standing quietly behind me said, "I've had a cramp right here." She touched a spot low in her abdomen.

These girls had developed a devilish look. Their tone of voice had gotten smoother, more sensual. I glanced over at Pat, he rolled his eyes a bit; this was going to be interesting. I gently palpated the spot she had indicated. No point or rebound tenderness, no history of pregnancy or bleeding (in fact she volunteered she was on the pill.) "I'm not ready to have a baby. I'm a *Sport* model" she said with a quiet giggle.

Pat cut in, "If you girls feel bad then make sure you see your Doctor. Doesn't look like you need the Paramedics."

"What are you guys going to do now?" the brunette asked.

"Well, we've got to go out on other calls, there are people out there having heat attacks and getting shot; all that stuff" I said.

"Can't you stay a while?" they said in stereo. Pat and I glanced at each other, we knew this had potential, *big* potential, positive and negative. But, being the professionals we were, and both of us being happily married, well, *married*; we would do the right thing.

I looked the cute brunette right in the eye and said. . .

"Are you a model? I noticed these pictures." I pointed to the wall.

"Yes I am, here look at these" she moved into a nearby bedroom and motioned me to follow. On the wall were a half dozen 8x10's of her and her cute smile, and nothing else.

"This is nice" I said. It looked like the Caribbean. A gentle wave was breaking at her waist, she was frozen with her arms up, her wet breasts full and inviting, her nipples hard, and that little smile.

"This one is from *Penthouse*." She pointed to a collage of magazine pages, "September 78.'"

"*Really* nice" I said. I could hear Pat in the living room entwined in a conversation with the brunette's friend.

I heard the girl in the living room say something about skinny dipping and women with large breasts. It was time to make my move. It was us and them, alone, primed and willing, irresistible... well, nearly.

"We've got to get going..." I said to the girl. "Pat!" I called out as I hurried into the living room. I punched the alarm test button on my watch and called out... "We've got a run." I looked at my wrist, pretending I had some sort of *James Bond/Dick Tracey* radio watch and looked at Pat. "It's a shooting. You girls take it easy, bye."

We were half way down the hall when the brunette called out something like, "Come back if you can."

"O.K., bye, bye" I said.

As we drove away Pat said, "It's a good thing we're straight shooters."

"Yeah" I said. I guess he meant we did the right thing.

I often wonder what 'could' have happened that warm summer night in Hollywood, and it's better I think, imagining. Picturing that smile, the wave breaking at her waist, and blending bits and pieces of fact and fiction for use in my 'Tall tale' file.

Chapter Twenty-Four
Frankenstein

How about the day we ran over the guy.

He was on PCP. He was there standing on the curb as we pulled up in front of the house. "Did you call?" I said, from my half-opened window. His head turned slowly, mechanically, his eyes were wide and empty. I could see his eye balls twitching rapidly from side to side, *Nystagmus*. That, coupled with his Frankenstein imitation as he headed toward me was enough to switch to red alert. "Let's go" I yelled to my partner as I tried to roll up the window. Too late, he was on us, literally. His left hand held on to the top of my window, it was open about two inches. His right hand held the front red waning light on the hood, and he was biting the antenna. He began to pound the windshield.

"Knock him off" I yelled to my partner.

"How?"

"Go forward then slam on the brakes!"

We began jerking forward and back trying to dislodge the lunatic. He was beating the windshield and growling. Blood was trickling from his mouth and the antenna was bent. By now he'd also ripped off the red light on the front hood of the ambulance, it was waving back and forth hanging from its wires, casting an ominous intermittent red glow on Frankenstein's face.

"Knock him off!" I ordered.

"O.K., hold on."

My partner was serious now, we were going about 30 miles per hour in reverse when he locked up the wheels.

Frankenstein disappeared. We clicked into *Drive* and creeped forward... thump... thump. We bounced up and down in our seats. We looked nervously at each other. Frankenstein! I opened my door and looked back. There he was... dead in the street.

Well, he *looked* dead. "Grab your light" I told my partner. I snatched my five-cell metal *'Streamlight'* from the door holder. It was a nice light, but it would make a great *club* to beat Frankenstein to death if I had to.

We walked back and slowly approached the body. He growled. A black and white pulled up just then. I explained about the monster while my partner gave him a quick, but careful, check. He was fine. The police took him away and transported him to County Jail Ward, which also had a medical team.

So, Frankenstein appeared no worse for the ordeal. "No harm no foul." The tread marks on his pants would come out with a good washing, and maybe some *'Spray n' wash.'*

But *we'd* suffer for this. Our ambulance was broken, well the antenna and the light, but it meant we'd have to 'change over' into another ambulance, which meant a long drive downtown, and us moving *all* our equipment into the replacement ambulance. It would be a *long* night. Thanks Frankenstein.

Chapter Twenty-Five
Her Majesty, the Queen.

What had begun as a routine injury call would become an unforgettable piece of the tapestry which makes up my life as an L.A. City Paramedic, and a tidbit for idle moments in conversation.

When I saw him sitting there on the curb, holding his leg, dressed in his 'English Beefeaters' outfit, I had a vision. He was no longer a parking attendant for the *Century City Hotel*, he was a Royal Guard for Her Majesty the Queen of England.

As we headed toward *L. A New Hospital* I briefed the man on his role in the drama which was about to unfold. He laughed. He was ours.

We rolled the gurney quickly through the doors of the E.R. My partner and I threw a fragment of conversation toward the first Nurse we passed. Without looking at her, or addressing her directly, the effect would be an earful of eavesdropped chatter.

"Make the gurney up later, let's get out of here. The press will be right behind us" I said.

"The Queen is coming too" my partner added.

"Did you say the press is coming?" She had nibbled the bait.

"Yeah, he's a Royal Guard for the Queen of England."

My partner chimed in, "It was a Zoo out there, he's the Queen's personal guard and she was very upset, she's coming here."

"You're kidding, right?" she mused. This was the moment of truth, it was make it or break it time.

"No, we're not kidding. The Queen is at the Century City Hotel meeting with the Reagan's (the news had widely covered the President's visit to L.A. and his arrival in Century City earlier in the day) "She's on her way here to check on her guard, it's going to be a mess of reporters, we're getting out of here quick."

We hurried past her, dead serious, an air of urgency about us. The Nurse hurried to the phone. She paged security to the E.R. STAT. The hook wasn't only bit, it was swallowed and the whole hospital was being reeled in.

As we hurried out of the emergency room the staff was buzzing. A Doctor was on the phone to the Director of the hospital, it was 1 a.m.

We kept our serious faces intact until we had pulled away. Hospital security was setting up at the entrance, and inside the flurry of activity was frightening. The Queen was on her way.

I don't know when they finally figured it out, and luckily neither of us worked regularly in this area, so we wouldn't have to face any of the staff any time soon.

Yes, it was cruel, but we had no choice. Sometimes these things take on a life of their own; there's no stopping them.

Chapter Twenty-Six
Happy Birthday

"**R**escue 81, Engine 81, respond to the OBS" reported as an imminent birth...

It's a common story, "I've been having contractions all day and my water broke four hours ago, and then I started to feel like I needed to push, but I figured I had enough time to do three loads of laundry, wax the kitchen floor, and shampoo the living room carpet..." Not this time.

She was on her back on the dining room floor, her legs were spread wide. She moaned painfully with each contraction. The top of the baby's head bulged out, she was ready and this baby wasn't going to wait.

Her husband was holding her hand and coaching her on her breathing, he let us know they had taken *Lamaze* classes and that they wanted a *natural* birth.

My partner handed the Fireman a 1000cc bag of Normal Saline and a Maxi-drip tubing set up while he began to gather the IV catheter, alcohol wipes, tape and tourniquet.

"What's that stuff for?" the husband asked.

"We need to start an intravenous line in case we need to give her medications or replace fluids."

"No IV's and no drugs. We're going to have a natural birth." He said sternly.

Another groan of pain and the baby's head began to deliver. I had my size 8 surgical gloves on and placed the palm of one hand on top of the protruding skull, while the fingers of my other hand worked around the circumference between Mom and the baby. My job was three fold; prevent a too rapid (explosive) delivery by applying firm pressure against the head, prevent a tearing of the skin being stretched during delivery by carefully guiding over-stressed areas past the baby, and one of the most important and potentially dangerous concerns was that of detecting a problem with the umbilical cord, either prolapsed (coming out in front of the baby and being pinched off from the pressure) or a cord which had encircled the baby's neck, making delivery impossible and strangling the child in the process (in this emergency the cord would have to be cut quickly.)

This was different, the baby's head was face down, by this time in the birth process the baby generally should have rotated sideways, its face to one side, shoulders aligned vertically. The top shoulder can be guided out by tilting the baby's head downward, and then the bottom shoulder clears the pelvis with a gentle lifting of the head. This facilitates movement through the birth canal and the child is then easily delivered. I worked my fingers in more deeply. Another contraction, the baby's head turned slightly, and I could feel the top shoulder pressing tightly against the birth canal and could feel the baby's fingers next to its neck, its arm was folded upward.

The Mother grimaced as I pushed my hand deeper. I tried to fold the arm down or push the shoulder back, no luck. I quickly explained the problem to my partner. The father seemed to sense the urgency.

"What do you do now?" he asked.

I spoke over my shoulder to the fire Captain, making a statement and answering the father at the same time "If we can't deliver the baby in the next minute we're going to transport code 3 to Holy Cross, we need a driver."

"You got it." He quickly picked a fireman to drive the rescue and had the gurney placed behind us.

The Mother was on oxygen by mask and my partner continued his attempts at convincing the husband to allow an IV. "Look, this is an emergency now, we're going to start an IV, O.K.?" He placed the tourniquet on her arm.

The wife looked up, sweat poured from her forehead "Let em honey" she said weakly.

"All right, go ahead, but no drugs unless you have to."

The line was quickly established and taped in place. The baby's head was delivered as far as the neck. He was blue, and stuck, and the mother's contractions had stopped. He seemed like a *big* baby, and he was *really* stuck.

Both of my hands were half way inside her as we rolled down the driveway and into the ambulance. My partner got on the radio and relayed the urgency of the situation to the Hospital, and told them "We're five minutes out."

"Roger, do what you can, we'll set up for you, let us know if anything changes. We'll be on the radio, but we'll leave you alone, we know you've got your hands full."

"Roger, Holy Cross."

"Come on!" I urged as I pulled on the little arm. I felt a cold chill as I pushed and pulled against the baby's body, he was in big trouble, he was dying. I had to get him out, the cord was against his body just out of reach, I could feel it with my finger. If I could relieve some of the pressure on it, and if the placenta was still properly attached, we could keep him alive.

I reached deeper, I was hurting the mother, and I had few choices now. I pulled firmly on the baby's head. I could just barely hook my finger under his arm pit but couldn't grip enough to pull. Her contractions continued but weaker now, the baby wasn't moved by the contractions anymore.

I thought "What if I pull too hard and damage his neck, what if I paralyze this kid?" I knew he was dying. I pushed his shoulder again and hard. I was the only one talking "Come on, come on, move!" My partner and the fireman riding in the back could only watch and reassure the mother; it was up to me.

We were about three minutes to the E.R. I thought I would hurt him, I mean really hurt him, but I *had* to deliver him, it had been too long. Maybe he was brain damaged already? Maybe I hadn't done enough? I decided to move his shoulder, even if I had to break his collar bone or dislocate the shoulder. I was going to deliver this baby and do it now. My partner suctioned the mouth and nose again. I told the mother to "Push hard!" The mother let out a strained and muffled scream as I pushed then pulled hard with both hands, my foot was braced against the gurney arm rail.

The baby's body twisted sideways, the top shoulder shifted down, I pulled forward on the bottom shoulder.

"Oh god!" shouted the mom as her baby was pulled from her.

He was blue, all blue, he didn't move. My partner had placed two towels across my lap and held another one. I quickly placed the baby face down across my lap, grabbed the towel and rubbed his tiny body vigorously. My partner was flicking the baby's feet, hard. We knew if we couldn't stimulate him to breathe within a few more seconds we would have to breathe for him, and that the lack of spontaneous breathing was a really bad sign. "Breathe, breathe" I said over and over.

"We're a minute out" the driver yelled.

His cry was weak at first, his face began to turn pink, and then his arms. He cried hard now, as I flicked the bottom of his foot again. I felt his little arms for signs of damage, they seemed O.K. He was moving his arms and legs and looked pretty good. I laid him across his mother's chest. She had tears in her eyes as she touched his tiny cheeks. He looked great, mom was fine, and I was exhausted.

"We're here" as we backed in close to the E.R. doors.

The staff met us outside; a Nurse, a Tech, and the Doc. "Hey you did it!" the Nurse called out as the doors were opened. I handed him all bundled up in a clean towel to the Nurse. He was looking around, almost smiling.

"Gee, he looks good" the Doc commented.

"We had a tough time back here" I said as I wiped my forehead. One look at me and they knew it had been a close one.

I stood there in the E.R. for about ten minutes, watching the Doctor examine the kid. With a hospital towel around my neck soaking up the perspiration, I looked a bit like a fighter after the twelfth round. I reminded the Doctor to take a special look at the baby's left shoulder and arm and explained how hard I had to pull and push to get him out. "He seems O.K., I don't see any problems there" the Doc reported.

"That's great, I was worried" I said as I headed to the break room to start the paperwork.

I found out later the baby was just fine and was home in two days. I kept the parents' phone number and gave them a call a couple of months later. The mom was very thankful and was glad to talk to me about it. It was good. We did a good job. Without us maybe he would have died. Happy birthday!

Chapter Twenty-Seven
Three hookers
and an inflatable doll

I recall a few years ago, we had gone to an old Fire Station in Hollywood to get gas.

I think the Station has since been demolished, it was old. Well anyway, while I was standing by the gas pump I noticed a van pull over to the curb across the street. The driver began talking to a *young lady* who had been walking down the street. It was 2 a.m.

After a brief conversation, the van parked and the 'lady' got in. Myself, my partner, and a Fireman had been watching the two, and simultaneously drew the same conclusion. The interior light came on in the back of the van, the side curtains were drawn shut, and within a few moments the van began to rock.

The Fireman got a big smile on his face and then, like a cat stalking a bird, he headed across the street. He peeked in through an open corner of the curtain then motioned us over. My partner and I looked at each other, decided that peeking in on other people's private activities was unprofessional and immature; and hurried across the street

I guess the Fireman's panting must have tipped them off, because about the time we had neared the van the curtain flew back and a smiling blonde with big brown eyes was staring at us. She looked at us, licked her lips, and then pulled the curtain closed again. Having been caught in the act we did an about face and went back to fueling up the Rescue. The Fireman admitted he couldn't really see anything from his angle anyway.

A few moments later the blonde hopped out, waved good-bye to the driver, and then waved good-bye to us.

That was Hollywood in 1983. It's been cleaned up a bit since then, but the blonde is probably still out there somewhere, and the peeping Fireman, he's since inflated the story to include three hookers, John Holmes, and an inflatable doll.

Chapter Twenty-Eight
To be 'Somebody'

Many Paramedics and Firemen in the L.A.F.D don't live in L.A. This is understandable after you've done this kind of work for a while.

Although you can find the same types of crimes and undesirable people in any city, you can find a lot more of them in L.A.

What happened in September 1990 in front of Fire Station 15, near USC, wasn't unusual for the area. What was unusual is that it happened right in front of the Fire Station, and less than ten feet from ten Firemen.

We had come back from a call about five minutes earlier, and were upstairs heading for bed. It was around 1 a.m. I heard the front doors of the Station open and the sound of Fire trucks backing in.

Suddenly a series of four shots exploded outside. It was close, 'real' close. I told my partner to 'suit up.' I slipped on my jumpsuit and headed for the pole hole. I looked down and could see the Fireman in the tiller bucket, he was ducked down in his seat, and his face was chalk white with fear.

"Is everybody all right?" I called down.

"We've got guys shot and people running around with guns, stay up there" he shouted.

At that point I thought some Fireman might be down. My partner and I cautiously made our way down the stairs. As we peeked around the comer at the end of the stairs I could see the Truck had stopped, backed part way into the Station. A blue four-door was smashed into the side of the firetruck and a Fireman was kneeling over a man crumpled in the gutter across the street. There were a half dozen strangers running down the street, and two or three walking around just *inside* the Fire Station. The Captain yelled over to me "The shooter's gone!" as my partner tossed me my bullet proof vest. We slipped the vests over our jumpsuits and made our way over spent shotgun shell casings to the other side of the street. The man, a 20-year-old Mexican, was coughing up blood. He was pale and flailing about, too confused to answer our questions.

"Can't palpate a pressure" said the Fireman who was kneeling beside the man. I was busy with my rescue scissors slicing off his shirt while my partner was shouting out instructions to the other Firemen nearby. We had him in a Mast suit and on the way in a couple of minutes. My partner had already tried for two IV sticks by the time we had gone three blocks.

"He's shut down, can't get it" as he switched the tourniquet to the other arm.

I was on the radio letting County Hospital know we were on the way.

"Rescue 15 from USC, be advised we are *closed* to trauma." The only chance this guy had was at a *Trauma Center*, getting his chest opened up and getting the bleeding stopped.

"USC from 15, we're four minutes to you, we have no other trauma center, this patient is going down quickly, we're coming to you."

"O.K. 15 sounds like you don't have much choice, see you in four, USC clear."

"Got it!" shouted my partner as he advanced the catheter of a 16 gauge IV. "Let's pump him up" he grabbed the bulb attached to the pressure gauge and began to squeeze. The inflating pressure bag began to squeeze against the 1000 cc saline. We were two minutes out now and had infused 500 cc. The patient was pale, his lips cyanotic, his eyes rolled back, he didn't respond to painful stimulus anymore. He looked like he was about to arrest. I reached down to feel his carotid pulse, it was weak and rapid, barely palpable. I doubted if they could save him now. "We're here" as we swung wide then backed into a spot between two other ambulances. It was a hectic night at 'The General.'

The back doors jerked open. I had unhooked the 02 and was holding the IV bag as the gurney was pulled out.

We walked quickly through the automatic double doors, then slid the E.R. curtains back.

"STAT ident. in C" I called out as we passed the triage desk.

"C" booth was the main trauma room at County Hospital. The most critical patients showed up there, and it's there that they would live or die. If they're lucky they'll be stabilized and rushed to surgery, the unlucky, who have no chance, undergo an assault of medical techniques and technologies at the hands of medical students there to learn, and are the subject of a lot of "Wow, look at this" and "Have you ever seen one of these before?" while the interns all file through for an impromptu anatomy lesson or to inspect some surgical technique. When the patient has offered up his particular contribution toward the education of a half dozen or so new Doctors, he's pronounced dead, and wheeled off to the morgue. The next patient isn't far behind, this time it was our patient who filled the temporary void in "C" booth. During the next 15 minutes, he became one of those nameless cadavers, and a late night lesson in chest tube placement and open cardiac massage.

He died there in "C" booth, just another gang-banger who was the victim of some rival gang. But he was somebody's son, a son who wanted to be 'somebody,' who felt important with his Homies, wearing the colors. A young man who would never get the chance to *really* be somebody.

Chapter Twenty-Nine
Christmas

Christmas Eve.

I was working at Fire Station 38. Working on major holidays is always a drag. My two-year-old twins were at home and I was at the Fire Station. I was more than a little depressed. I wanted to be home, sitting by the fireplace, looking at our Christmas tree. We had a nice tree this year...

I remember when I first got married, we couldn't afford a Christmas tree. I was working Christmas Eve, and noticed as the tree lots closed down that many of the best, most expensive trees, were left unsold, doomed to spend their Christmas toppled over in the dirt, their purpose in life unfulfilled.

Driving past one of those lots I told my partner to pull over. As we walked around in the closed lot among all those grand and beautiful trees, guilty only of being too big or too expensive, I knew that *this* Christmas we would have a Christmas tree; the best and biggest tree ever.

I picked an eight-foot beauty. It barely fit as we laid it atop the gurney, its perfect top picking up a defibrillator paddle in place of an Angel, as we shoved and pushed and quickly slammed the back doors. We hurried back to the station, making plans as we drove in case we got a call. We would lay it on someone's lawn then retrieve it afterward; that would work, no problem.

We made it back without a call. I quickly transferred the noble giant to my VW Bug. The trunk protruded out the passenger window, and I doubted if our Angel at home would stay attached to the bent and twisted tree top, but felt better the rest of the shift knowing we'd have a Christmas tree this year.

I decided I could make it home without using the rear or right side mirrors, and would *probably* be able to shift. I didn't usually use the right half of the windshield anyway, and I could always scoot forward a little, the steering wheel against my ribs wouldn't hurt *that* much.

I think it was my improved mood after the tree napping that prompted my call to OCD that night. We were coming back from a run when it hit me. As my partner sleepily steered us back toward quarters I picked up the microphone.

"OCD, we need two Task Forces, four RA's, a Chief and the PD for traffic control. We've got a sleigh into the side of the First Interstate Building, we've got Reindeer all over the street, it's a mess."

There was a long silence.

The broadcast had gone out to every Rescue ambulance and Fire truck on the street in Los Angeles. My partner was doubled up laughing; I thought he was choking to death. I heard OCD key the mike, then pause, I wondered what comeback they would offer.

Muffled laughter was broadcast from the dispatch center for about 10 seconds, then, "Roger, Rescue."

We decorated the tree as soon as I got home, about 8:30 Christmas morning, and had one of our best Christmases ever.

Chapter Thirty
Hiroshima chicken

Firehouse cooking has a mystique about it.

It is widely held that many a gourmet meal is prepared behind those doors, and that Firemen rival the World's finest Chefs. This is partly true, at least the part about Fire Station cooking having a certain mystique. In all fairness, there are some good cooks behind those doors, *some* good cooks. The rest are definitely out there trying to live up to the expectations placed on them. They go about it by concocting their own exotic delicacies with *improvements* to the cookbook recipes, which make their creations *unique*.

One favorite of mine is "Hiroshima Chicken." That's any standard chicken recipe that's either grilled, Bar-B-Que'd, roasted, broasted, baked, or micro-waved at least ten times longer than the recipe calls for. It comes crispy, extra crispy, and *nuclear waste*.

When it comes to chili, Firemen have an unwritten rule. The chili must be hot enough to cause immediate and profuse perspiration over the eater's entire body, temporary blindness, and fainting followed by coma. If all that doesn't occur after the first spoonful, then the cook must immediately dump one more cups of chopped jalapenos and/or chili powder into the already deadly mixture. Firefighters, in order to perpetuate their 'macho' image, always ask for the cayenne pepper, and add more while saying something like, "What is this stuff *Gerber's* baby food chili or what?" All while sweating, turning bright red, and losing most of their peripheral vision. So much for Firehouse cooking.

I've developed a little rule for myself after my years in the Fire Department, and try to follow it always, "Never eat anything that eats your spoon first."

Note: To you brand new EMT's or Paramedics who are sometimes in the rotation to be "The Cook"...

In my Department, the Paramedics were usually NOT in the cooking rotation. We were just too busy to be reliable cooks able to prepare and serve a meal on time. Many stations had a 'Permanent Cook' who had *actual* skill at cooking. But, at one station at least, the Paramedics were in the rotation, and it was *my* turn.

Now I swear I didn't plan this, and first of all, I'm NOT a good cook; I'm a *Kraft* Macaroni and Cheese sort of cook. Anyway, I went shopping. I planned on a nice and simple meal of ham and peas and instant mashed potatoes. I knew that the canned hams were already cooked, so I'd just have to *warm it up*. And peas, and instant potatoes, well *that's* easy.

To make a long story short, this station was a *Task Force*, which was the Rescue Ambulance, an Engine, and a Ladder Truck; which was about a *dozen* people. I figured I'd gotten *plenty* of food to feed all of them. The ham looked pretty big, it was a BIG can. And the peas, well I bought *four* bags of them, BIG bags. And I made more mashed potatoes than anyone could possibly eat. Everyone would get a nice slice of ham and lots of peas and potatoes, wonderful!

I realized we were in trouble when I opened the oven door, and discovered that the big ham had shrunk a bit. Maybe I over-cooked it, I don't know. But that *big* ham, for those dozen hungry firemen, was a little tiny ham-lump about 3" by 4", oops.

Everybody got a tiny, itty-bity, 'sliver' of ham, and a HUGE mound of peas, and a MOUNTAIN of potatoes, plus seconds or thirds or fourths of the peas and potatoes if they wanted them.

I wasn't asked to cook again, *ever*.

Chapter Thirty-One
...come to the pole hole.

The day they "bucketed' Cindy Garvey.

Bucketing. It's done something like this; a voice over the PA system, "Johnson, Johnson, come to the front pole hole." When Johnson, who must be a rookie since nobody with time on would fall for this obvious ploy, steps beneath the pole hole, the Firemen on the second floor, at the top of the pole hole, release the contents of their three buckets of water onto Johnson's head. It's great fun, except for Johnson.

There are hundreds of scenarios to lure the victim to the target zone, and once bucketed you have an obligation, no, a sacred duty, to bucket at least a half dozen others for revenge. It's logarithmic. Needless to say, in the 200+ year history of the L.A. City Fire Department, this had led to some poor souls being bucketed four or five times a day to keep up with the required pay backs. If you get too smart, and they can't trick you anymore, they just pull a hose into the station and attack you wherever you happen to be. There is no escape if they really *want you*.

A few years ago, the Fire Chief proclaimed that all "Water play" would cease immediately and added the threat of severe discipline; which equals days off without pay. Most water play came to a halt. One factor that hurried along the inevitable ban was the day *Cindy Garvey* visited Fire Station 35 in Hollywood.

Cindy was, maybe is, the wife of former *Dodger* baseball player Steve Garvey, and had gone to the station as part of some TV interview show she was doing. One of the Fireman had a brain storm, or maybe it was brain damage, but he figured it would be *really* funny to 'bucket' Cindy Garvey. Picture it, Cindy Garvey all dressed up in her $700 dress,

$200 hairdo, *bucketed*, now that's funny! When the fifteen gallons of water hit, it was clear that it *wasn't* funny, and that Fire Station humor may have a limited audience who fully appreciate it. Cindy *wasn't* one of those people.

The Garvey incident put an end to the old-time water wars. But time has a way of making memories fade. There's still a risk if you go to some fire station, that if you are called to a 'pole hole' or someone tries to get you to stand someplace outside the station for some reason, there is a chance a bucket is waiting somewhere above you. I hope you have an umbrella.

But now, generally, these days it's a more professional Fire Department. A department whose members realize they come to work to do a job and not to play. Employees of a City that expects a full day's work, and a businesslike demeanor.

I'll finish this chapter later. I've got to go put whipped cream inside my partner's pillow case.

Chapter Thirty-Two
"Officer down..."

Fire Station 98, the heart of Pacoima.

The red brick station stood square and bland on Van Nuys Boulevard, a fortress bearing the spray-painted scars of gang territory, but a safe haven for the neighborhood kids. The moms would walk their sons and daughters over to look at the firetrucks and ambulance, and to talk to the Paramedics and Firefighters. It was one of the few positive things in a neighborhood ravaged nightly by marauding gangs.

During my two years at 98's I had many of the *best* calls of my career. 'Best' in that they were memorable. Paramedics tend to use "good" when referring to calls they've handled as an adjective to describe what normal people would view as "bad." I guess it's understandable, it's our profession, the more terrible the situation the more chance you have to perfect your skills. Our work is one which accepts trying circumstances and difficult challenges as *positive* things. We are *supposed* to perform well under pressure, and the better Paramedics thrive on it.

There are many calls that nobody wants to go on. Injured children are universally bad calls to handle; innocent victims, vulnerable, helpless. If you have kids yourself I think it's worse, you identify with the sick or injured kids, and as a parent you tend to hurt along with them.

An injured coworker, friend, or family member presents the same problem; it's not the same when you know your patient, it's harder, it's personal.

We were "On the radio, in our first-in" a term describing our status as out of the Fire Station and available in our assigned service area. We were about two blocks from the station...

"Rescue 98 to a shooting, reported as an officer down, Lupine Avenue and Petri Place, Incident 736, at 12:34, OCD clear."

My partner's foot went to the floor, as he simultaneously flipped the light switch and turned the siren knob to "Wail." We knew the streets, we were three blocks away.

"Did they have an Engine with us?" I asked my partner.

"No it's just us" he replied.

I grabbed the mic. "OCD from 98, if this is an LAPD officer shot then send us an Engine company!"

First of all, most shootings require extra manpower, especially a policeman shot, with the potential for crowd control problems, and with the need for a driver to the hospital. My partner and I would be busy in the back taking care of the patient.

"Unbelievable" I shouted. "They'll send six Fire trucks, a Chief, and a Helicopter to a 'possible' house fire, and send us alone on a Policeman shot! Jesus!" (It was 1984).

As we passed our station the apparatus doors were opening, and the guys were running to the Engine.

"Watch for police cars" I reminded my partner.

Just then a police car going Code 3 skidded around the comer in front of us, then took a quick right at the next block.

We switched off the siren and turned the comer behind the Police car. Three Black & Whites were already on scene. Two of them had skidded sideways and stopped partly blocking the side street where the Officer lay next to his motorcycle.

My partner was first to him. I threw the MAST suit box down next him and looked up briefly. The other Police officers were stringing up yellow barricade tape, interviewing someone in their front yard, and another was talking on his car radio. None of them had done anything. Even though it was one of their own, they knew he was gone.

My partner cut open the uniform shirt. I threw his leather motorcycle jacket to an officer nearby; it was bloody and had at least two holes in the chest. Another officer reached over and grabbed the portion of the shirt with the badge attached.

"He's fixed and dilated" my partner called out. "No carotid" he added. My partner tossed me the Ambu-bag and began chest compressions. I started to ventilate as the Engine Company turned the corner.

"Shit" I heard from one of the Firemen as he ran up from behind. "I'll get the MAST suit on him" he said. He pulled the device under the officer's legs and hips and began pushing on the foot pump.

"Let's go" I said. "Tillson you drive, we're going to Mercy Medical."

"You got it" he said.

"Let's go, *now*!" I ordered. Three of us lifted him on the gurney.

He had a bullet wound to his neck, we placed a Vaseline gauze over it as the siren wailed. Tillson was a good driver, he was fast but safe. I didn't have to worry about us getting there in one piece.

Mercy Hospital was close by. I called ahead on the H.E.A.R. radio. "Mercy, Rescue 98, we're a minute and a half to you, we've got an LAPD officer in full arrest, multiple gunshots to the chest and neck, set up to crack his chest, we've got a Normal Saline open wide and the MAST suit is up, he's in asystole."

"What do you think?" one of the Firemen asked me.

"He's fucked" I said.

We were met at the door by the entire E.R. staff, they acted like they didn't believe it when I told them to be ready to crack his chest. The Doc looked rattled "Get the Thoracotomy tray open!" he screamed.

The staff knew him, he was a young officer, and he'd been in the E.R. for coffee that morning. "It's Tony" said one of the technicians. It took a little too long to open his chest, but it was only a drill. He didn't have a chance.

He didn't have his bullet proof vest on that morning, it probably would have saved him.

The Doctor was reaching into the Policeman's chest and squeezing his heart for circulation when I left the room.

He was a motorcycle cop. He pulled a car over for rolling through a stop sign. A quick ticket and they would be on their way. But one of the men in the car was wanted, and when the officer went back to his motorcycle he figured he was had. He got out of the car and fired. The officer fell and tried to reach for his gun. The man walked up to him and finished him off.

I went to the funeral. His wife and young son were there. The eulogies were very nice, and yes he was a hero. His job was to protect us.

I think of him when I hear somebody bad-mouthing the Police. I think of his young son and his wife, crying in that cemetery full of hundreds of people. And as I looked at them both, and as the Bag Pipers wailed *Amazing Grace*, I knew they were so very alone.

Chapter Thirty-Three
The Cat Lady

The *Cat Lady* used to hang out around *California Hospital*. She pushed a shopping cart and had a dozen or so cats tied to it with rope and string leashes.

She wore a black veil over her head and face; layers of black material formed a sort of robe/dress outfit. She never showed her face. There were a half dozen different stories about her. Some said she had tried to save four kids from a burning apartment, and was burned and disfigured in the attempt. Others said she was an eccentric millionaire who owned a string of nearby apartments.

I was working with Ray, my new partner. He was a bit strange, so it didn't surprise me when he said he wanted to go over and talk with the Cat Lady. We pulled the ambulance up to the curb and rolled down the window.

"Hi, where are all your cats?" Ray asked.

We had heard that someone had complained, and that the SPCA had taken her cats away. She had since gathered five more.

"They're gone" she said through the veil. "A lady brought me this." She pulled a crumpled bag of *Friskies* from the cart. I figured it would be difficult to keep them fed, and several of the felines looked a bit anorectic.

"Must be hard to..." I started to say.

"Want some chocolate" she interrupted. She pushed aside some empty Pepsi cans and produced a wad of aluminum foil.

Carefully and methodically she unwrapped the treat and held it out. The small hunk of gnawed-on chocolate appeared to be a well-aged specimen. I wondered for a minute, if like cheese or fine wine this chocolate could be in its prime. I don't know if it was the chocolate's 'bouquet' or the cat's, but I suddenly lost my appetite. "No thanks, we just ate."

"Want some coffee" she pried up the plastic lid then held out the rusty coffee can. About an inch deep of disguising tan liquid sloshed at the bottom. I was ready to ~~heave~~ leave. Ray was getting a kick out of her.

"Get your camera" Ray said. "Can I get a picture with you?" She stood there obligingly. Ray actually put his arm around her, although the black and white picture in my locker captured a grimace he couldn't hide.

Chapter Thirty-Four
Dad's gun

God how you wish you could make it all better.

We were only there for 15 or 20 minutes, we could walk away from it. The family would carry the pain forever, and I guess in a lesser way so would we.

A five-year-old boy stood on the front lawn and waved to us as we pulled up. He had been crying.

"What happened?" I asked him.

"My brother blew his head off" he said flatly and pointed toward the open front door.

"Is anybody else home?" I asked him.

"No, my mom went to the store."

"Stay right here, I'll be right back."

The five-year-old stood on the porch as my partner and I entered the house.

Cookie monster was bright and blue and loud on the living room T.V. "Cookies! Cookies! More Cookies!" You could smell the smoke in the hallway. There in the first bedroom, his parent's bedroom, lay the body of the 12-year-old boy. The shotgun was on the closet floor near his feet. Blood and pieces of bone and brain were blown throughout the large walk-in closet. Scattered over all the suits and dresses, the ties and the stockings, was all that remained of most of their son's head. The little brother was right.

My partner went out to the ambulance to call the police. I sat on the porch with the little boy. I asked the boy what had happened. He told me how his big brother was upset because he didn't want to shoot the shotgun with his Dad, he didn't like the noise. Dad didn't understand and was angry with him.

Bert and Ernie were flying kites when big brother came in and told his brother he could have all his toys, because he was going to go 'blow his head off.' Little brother thanked him, and asked if he could even have his GI Joe.

"Sure you can have everything" he said.

"Thanks a lot!" he said and turned back to watch The Grouch.

"Just leave me alone, the sign says DO NOT DISTURB" as Oscar slammed the trash can lid.

"Boom!" the windows rattled and smoke drifted from the bedroom. Little brother ran in and found him.

It would be hard for him to play with those toys, even the GI Joe. They just wouldn't seem so important after today, not even to a five-year-old.

As I sat on the porch with him, waiting for the Police, I tried to explain it. "Sometimes people get so upset and so confused and so hurt that they do something like this" I said. "You need to remember if you ever feel that way you can talk to somebody about it, you can solve any problem if you just tell your parents or any other adult and let them help you figure out what to do about it."

Just then a car pulled quickly into the driveway. "Mom!" the boy called out and began to cry.

"Billy!" she screamed, looking past the boy toward the house. "What happened!" she screamed to me and started to run. I stopped her near me.

"You don't want to go in right now, your son killed himself with the shotgun." There just wasn't a good way to say it.

"No!" she howled "No!" She ran next door to her neighbor, who was standing on the porch. The neighbor held her and took her inside.

I picked up the little boy. "Everything will be alright; it's just going to take some time for everybody. It'll be all right." But I knew it wouldn't be all right. This day would never be all right, and it would change *everything*. I held him tight. He looked up at me holding back the tears. "You can cry, it's O.K. to cry." He put his head on my shoulder and cried. I took a deep breath and held him close, he cried for both of us.

Chapter Thirty-Five
The beauty of radio

The van had overturned and slid 100 feet on its side, finally slamming into a tree on the sidewalk.

The driver may have been unconscious after the impact, or trapped in his seat by the twisted wreckage. In any case, the van exploded in flames, leaving the driver's body a charred, grotesque figure clutching the steering wheel.

We arrived as the news van's door flew open. The two men headed over to us. A Fire truck pulled up just then and began a quick attack on the fire. The van was completely engulfed in flames. A thick pillar of black smoke rose high into the night sky.

There was nothing we could do, not for this patient.

"Hey guys, what happened here?" the microphone was pushed forward.

"Don't put this on the air, you know as much as we do" I said. The microphone was tucked away and the tape recorder switched off. "The guy is fried in there, see him?" I pointed out the charred corpse to the news man, whose name I recognized from his press pass. He did the helicopter traffic reports. "Where's your whirlybird?" I asked.

"At Van Nuys for maintenance, but watch this."

I stood there waiting as his partner spoke into a small walkie-talkie. He handed the radio to the news man saying "20 seconds."

He turned toward us and placed the microphone to his mouth. "Listen to this" he said with a smile.

"This is Rob Curr, News radio Skywatch. We're in 'Skywatch 2' flying over the intersection of Overland and National. An orange plume of flame and smoke is boiling hundreds of feet into the air, below a man has died, burned to death after his van overturned and plowed into a tree. The Fire Department is on scene, we can see the smoke turn grey then white as the water begins to hit the flames. This is a tragic scene. The traffic northbound on Overland is at a standstill, looks like it'll be tied up for some time as attempts to extinguish the fire continues, and with the Coroner's investigation that will follow. From the scene of tragedy here in West L.A., this is Rob Curr Skywatch News, back to you."

"What'd ya think?" he asked me.

"You could have at least pounded your chest as you talked, or played helicopter noises" I said jokingly.

"When you've been a pilot as long as I have, you tend to think at altitude, it's like poetic license."

"O.K. you're forgiven, this time." I said. We both laughed as we turned away. Just then the blinding lights from a T.V. News camera team hit me. Oh, the beauty of radio.

Chapter Thirty-Six
What are you going to do when you grow up?

"You'll never work as a Paramedic again.

You had better decide what you want to do when you grow up." I was only 37. The doctor was direct and to the point. The MRI told the story. As an Orthopedic surgeon evaluating my injury, his job now was to write the report and list my restrictions. "This isn't something I would suggest surgery for, not yet anyway. You can't lift any significant weight or bend over, and you definitely can't work as a Paramedic. It's time to choose a new career, and do it quick. I'd suggest you see a worker's compensation attorney."

That was it. I'd never work as a Paramedic again. I looked over at my wife and crinkled up my mouth; she looked at me full of a hundred thoughts and questions. The doctor started to leave the room, but turned and said, "Let me know on December 3."

We'd have a month to think this all over, and consult the Attorney on how to proceed from here. Meanwhile I'd have regular physical therapy in an attempt to relieve pressure on the ruptured lumbar disc. No matter what the results of the therapy were, the best I could hope for was to relieve some of the pain, and to keep the disc from rupturing into the spinal column, forcing me into surgery, surgery which held no guarantee of relieving the pain. I had a bum back and could never do the job again, period.

I'd been off work since October 9th. I hurt my back lifting a patient a few days earlier, but kept working, thinking it would get better.

I wondered about the man I carried down the stairs that first week in October. He was in *congestive heart failure* when we arrived, with fluid filling his lungs, he would die without quick intervention. We assisted his breathing with our BVM, started an IV, and administered Morphine and Lasix. He was in bad shape.

I felt a tug and pain in my low back halfway down the stairs. By the time we pulled into the hospital he was doing better. He would survive this time.

He'd never know about me. How my career as a Paramedic came to an end that October morning. I hope he did well, he was the *reason* I became a Paramedic.

Eleven years and three months. How many patients had I treated? How many lives had I touched and had touched mine? Conservatively, in 135 months, at 10 shifts per month, (plus some significant overtime) and an average of 10 calls per shift (I know my average was much more). That works out to somewhere in the neighborhood of 15,000 calls in my career.

How many lives had I saved? It would be safe to say *hundreds*. More often than not we would never know our patient's outcome. Our job ended when the hospital took over. Of course the reverse is true, the patient never really knew who had 'saved' them.

It was part of a general perception, and an accurate one, that EMT's and Paramedics save lives. Our thanks was knowing we had done our best. The rare "Thank you" was nice, but we didn't do it for that. We became EMT's and Paramedics to make a difference in someone's life, to be there when tragedy struck, to reach out, to care, to do a good job.

To that man who couldn't breathe that afternoon in October, I'm glad I could help. You're welcome.

Chapter Thirty-Seven
Sometimes in a dream

We got the call after the fire had been put out. We arrived to find the smoldering burned out hulk of a large motorhome on the shoulder of the freeway.

For several hundred feet behind it, a burn-marked line traced a path from where the fire started to here. Several cars had pulled over to help. Two people had used their small fire extinguishers and tried in vain to put out the fire. We bandaged the burned hand of a young man and listened to the story he told.

We stepped through the smoldering debris and over a charred body in the walkway, back to a side rear window. The little burned body was propped up, toward the window, propped in the charred remains of outstretched arms.

The smell of burned flesh lingered as I sat in the Rescue and filled out the three D.B. (Dead Body) reports. The bystanders had watched it, the last terrible moments as they died. They did what they could, tried to put out the fire, screamed to them to "jump out" of the doorway through the flames; they did what they could.

I had a dream that night, I saw it all...

Jennifer was just learning to walk, Grandma tried to keep her from standing. The bouncing motorhome wasn't the best training ground for a new walker.

"That girl needs sleep Margaret" her husband urged from the driver's seat. They were playing A,B,C blocks on the table.

"Frank, how far to Fresno?"

"We've got a ways to go, the turn off to interstate 5 is up ahead."

A tremendous 'Pop' and a loud hissing sound startled everybody. The baby started to cry.

"What was that!" Frank yelled as he took his foot off the gas.

"A tire, maybe?" Margaret called out. She set the baby in the small playpen and headed up front. The motorhome was slowing as she walked past the kitchen area.

"Frank! There's a fire!" she yelled. The smoke began to pour inside from under the floor. "Frank!"

As he pulled over the flames grew, the smoke blocked his view out the windshield, he swerved toward the shoulder.

"Frank!"

"Stay back Margaret!" He pulled the emergency brake, the motorhome skidded the last 10 feet to a stop. "Jesus!" he yelled as he unclipped the small fire extinguisher next to his seat. "Margaret!" he screamed as he emptied the white powder into the flames. The smoke was too thick to see.

"Jump out the door!" a man screamed to the Grandma. He could see her there, she was holding the baby. The flames blocked the door, she'd have to run through them to get out. "Jump out!" the voice pleaded. She turned and headed to the rear of the motorhome, to the side window.

Grandpa fell inside as the hot smoke burned deep into his lungs. The flames spread quickly. Hot black smoke and flames puffed from the side window as Grandma pushed her granddaughter toward it.

The news described it as a "Terrible tragedy" and the bodies as being burned beyond recognition. It was terrible, but as for the bodies, I knew them. Grandma, Grandpa, and the baby. I still see them, sometimes in a dream…

The motorhome pulls up to a small home in Fresno. Grandpa honks the horn and waves to the young man mowing the front lawn. The side door swings open, Grandma is holding the baby's little hand.

"Look how she learned to walk!" Grandma beams.

They say you can glimpse Heaven in a dream. I hope so.

Chapter Thirty-Eight
Like a Beacon

I used to drive out of my way to pass the motorcycle shop at Roscoe Street and Winnetka Boulevard. The black 1978 BMW 750cc motorcycle sat there all shiny in the center of the floor.

I stood there, nose pressed against the glass, studying the curve of the gas tank. The square white price tag hung there by a string, swinging from the handle bar like a beacon. That BMW sat there week after week, waiting; with my name on it.

It's a longer story but... my boss had the secretary put down I had worked there for a year and a half, although it had only been six months. From the day I first saw it there I knew I'd have it, it had my name on it. I bought that BMW motorcycle. Thank God for Capitalism and falsified credit applications. This Chapter won't be an example of proper morals and ethics I guess, but when I got that BMW I wasn't a Paramedic yet, I got better.

The first call of the day. It was a beautiful, crisp, blue, morning. The February air bit as I rolled down my window to the man waving in the street.

"He's dead, he's there at the corner, right there" he pointed toward the end of the block; there were two other people standing there.

We pulled up and stopped near the body lying there in the dirt... A biker: "Born to ride" was blazed across the back of his black leather jacket. He was probably 40, and balding.

His skull was cracked open, missing from just below his left eye in a wide 'V' shape across half his forehead and disappearing into an empty black cavity where the back of his head should be. His Harley was at least twenty feet away, at the end of a long serpentine trail in the dirt

He lost it at the apex of a sweeping downhill turn. The path in the dirt paralleled a chain link fence as he tried to recover. It was the fence post at the next turn that did him in. Looked like he hit it head first.

He didn't look like the type to wear a helmet if he could help it. Although a helmet wouldn't have done much for this guy, except to maybe keep his brains close by. They sat there, fat and perfect, several feet away, enough to bring tears to the eyes of any scarecrow, steaming in the cool morning air.

There's no punch line, no lesson really. Except maybe the realization that the picture of that morning, the bite of the air as I watched the steam rise, and that gruesome scene, is as clear now as on that February morning all those *years* ago.

Chapter Thirty-Nine
"Stupid"

He didn't deserve to have battery acid explode in his face, no one deserves that. *Deserving* is definitely not the right word, "Stupid" that's the word.

It was about 10:30 on a Saturday night. He'd been working on his car all day. After hours of cranking the tired old 63' Impala engine, the 'Die Hard' finally died. Jose' was a pretty good mechanic. He had kept that old Chevy going for years; he had a knack for mechanical things. As far as *electrical* things go, Jose' could have used a *How-To* book or something. I mean a *lighted match* to look down in the little battery hole to check the water, geez! It exploded, yada, yada.

It's one thing to be stupid, but worse I think to have stupid friends, at least it was for the poor guy that summer, during a front yard Bar-B-Que.

He grabbed that can of charcoal lighter and began to soak down the coals. This sucker was gonna light with 'one' match. He squeezed that can and squeezed that can, he soaked each and every little coal. His reputation as the Grand Master of front lawn Bar-B-Que's would remain intact. His buddies watched every move. They laughed and ou'd and aw'd and applauded and guzzled more *Budweiser*. The stream of lighter fluid danced and swirled at the hands of the master, it was art, it was sheer beauty.

The moment of truth.

Just when you think you're in control, when everything is going as planned, when your next step is carefully orchestrated, and timed to a tee. Well, the King of the front yard Bar-B-Que was like that, he was a pro. His hand plunged into his pocket to retrieve some matches. His smile grew. His buddies watched and burped in anticipation. Then, from behind, a rebel can of Budweiser (there's always one bad can) grabbed someone's hand, struck a match and let it fly. The Bar-B-Que King didn't have a chance, no time to back up.

The mushroom cloud could be seen for miles, the King burst into flames.

Every kid learns it, "Stop-Drop-and Roll."

The King was no kid, he was 38 years old, he screamed and began to run. His inebriated buddies hesitated, they could save him but... but... the 'Budweiser'? To save the King. . . what the hell.

They began to chase him around the yard dumping cold Budweiser's on him. The cans were popping furiously, the Budweiser brigade relayed the cans; from the cooler, past the picnic table, one after another.

He was extinguished when we arrived. If it had been a road runner cartoon it would have been *really* funny, but it wasn't a cartoon. The man had some serious burns. Large portions of skin were sluffing off his arms, back, and hands. He would require months and months and scores of skin grafts to recover.

Sometimes we joke about these things, but all the sick jokes and incidents we can laugh at later, they involved real people, people just like us. It's when I remember that, that it's just not funny anymore.

Chapter Forty
The carpet's moving

My house is often a mess. I can't help it. I end up building piles of mail and magazines and miscellaneous junk, I *feel* like I'm organized but, I'm NOT.

When the piles of important papers grow high enough, I throw them out. I can usually bump the vacuum into the piles and push them around enough to clean the floor. Other than the piles, it's just the normal collection of misplaced toys, errant dirty laundry, dishes waiting for the dishwasher, etc. That's my idea of a mess.

One thing my job has offered me is the opportunity to visit the homes of thousands of *different* people. People from all walks of life, of all races and cultures, and from every economic level of society. It still surprises me when I see the conditions that some people are willing to live in.

I recall examining a middle-aged mother one evening when suddenly I noticed the carpet was moving. I began to fidget a bit when I realized it was the thousands of creatures living *in* the carpet that were moving. Little hopping fleas wiggling into my socks, families of long brown cockroaches who's little one's played tag across my forearm.

Her kids sat there on that carpet, occasionally brushing a roach from their face or scratching their heads.

I took a long hot shower and changed my uniform as soon as we got back to the station, but itched and scratched and slapped myself the rest of the shift. I made a call to Child Protective Services. I hope they did the right thing.

My piles of junk looked good to me when I got home the next morning. I let them get a little higher now before I sort them out or throw them away. It could be worse.

Chapter Forty-One
Going, going, gone.

Suicides aren't funny, not the ones I've seen. But they are often interesting, either the reason for the deed, and often the method.

A young girl, 22 years old, decided to end it all. She carefully covered all the windows of the living room; I guess she didn't want anyone to peek in and stop her. Then she placed a six-foot step ladder in the center of the floor, climbed it, and tossed a long and beautiful hand macrame'd rope over a beam crossing the ceiling. She tied a noose around her neck and stepped off of the ladder. Oh yeah, she had flung a bath towel over the beam before tossing the rope across it. Her roommate would say later that she thought she did that so as not to mar the finish on the wood beam. It was that beautiful old beam that had attracted them to the house. How thoughtful.

Her roommate came in late that night. She headed across the room toward the light switch on the wall and smacked right into her. Her dead friend was swinging in big circles when she finally reached the light switch. She stumbled screaming to the phone to call 9-1-1. She stood right there in that living room staring at her friend until we arrived. I took her out into the kitchen to ask her the questions for my form. She was trembling. She told me she'd never be able to stay in that house, not now.

They'll never know, the new owners. They'll probably fall in love with that high ceiling and that beautifully finished wooden beam, just like new.

In a small neglected apartment, an obviously troubled and dangerous young man took his life. He was lying on the bed in his underwear. The shotgun was propped on his knees. A string went from the trigger, across the room, around the closet doorknob, and back to the young man's left hand. His right hand was holding his penis. A dozen boxes of shotgun shells were piled along the wall. A set of camouflaged fatigues lay on the floor. Luckily this fellow didn't decide to take his troubles to the streets.

His head, what was left of it, was turned toward the floor. His last vision of life on Earth was a *Playboy* center fold, having just dropped her tight white evening gown on the floor. Not a bad last vision.

Chapter Forty-Two
Three days

I was beginning a 72. That's three consecutive 24 hour shifts.

I used to do it quite a bit when I first came on the job, but avoided it at all costs these days. Even if you have relatively easy days you feel pretty much like a zombie after 72 straight hours. But, I wanted to get some extra money to buy tires for my car, and signed up for overtime stating "72's O.K." I was hoping for the best, but all three days were at busy stations.

Usually when I came home from work my wife would ask "What kind of calls did you have?" And I'd usually answer, "Same stuff, nothing big." Unless a plane crashed, or some other major or unusual event occurred, all the other stuff was run-of-the-mill. She had a hard time accepting that "nothing big" reply and wanted to hear what kind of calls I had, regardless of what they were. After a standard, basically uneventful shift, I really had trouble recalling those kinds of calls. I figured I'd be ready for her when I got home in three days. I'd hand her this list...

<u>DAY ONE</u>:

7:56 a.m. "Seizure" - A 25-year-old man. He was a mental patient who was also a diabetic and epileptic, he had had a seizure. He was at a board and care home with other mentally disturbed adults. One of the other borders had shoved a spoon in the man's mouth during the seizure (never put anything in a seizing person's mouth, the worse thing they'll do is bite their tongue and cut it up a bit, that's no big thing.) The spoon had broken out the man's front teeth (that's a big, and expensive, thing.) This man had frequent seizures, at least once a week, and was alert when we got there. We talked to his private doctor on the phone, and on the doctor's advice arranged a private ambulance to transport him to the hospital where his doctor was on staff.

9:30 a.m. "Woman down" - A 20-year-old hysterical woman. She had an argument with her boyfriend and was pretending to go in and out of consciousness. When we arrived, we got the story from the family, then went to the bedroom where she was laying sprawled out on the bed. No response to verbal or painful stimulus, although, her eyelids did flutter a little when I applied the specially modified and copyrighted "Simultaneous trapezius pinch, sternal rub, digital crunch, ocular nerve crush, and the (later outlawed) Nazi bicep twisting pinch." If we couldn't get her to talk to us, and make sure she was alert and oriented, we would have to take her to the hospital. We knew she was faking. Luckily this was a few years ago, and we could still use 'ammonia inhalants.' Snap one of these beauties under the nose of an upset 20-year-old feigning unconsciousness and, Eureka!

"Snap." She tried to turn away, we moved the inhalant as she moved. Within three seconds she was cursing at us and trying to hit me. But, she was alert and oriented, and gladly answered all our questions when we threatened to snap another ammonia capsule. We left her with her family. "Son of a bitches!" she called out as we left.

1:01 p.m. "Man down" - A nine-year-old boy, at school, who fell 10 feet from a tree when a branch broke. He seemed O.K., his back was sore. We bundled him up on a back board and took him to the hospital.

4:29 p.m. "Heart" - A 78-year-old diabetic man. Felt weak while doing yard work. Was pale, sweaty, cool and was having about 10 PVC's a minute. Started an I. V, gave 50cc or Dextrose (50% sugar.) The PVC's stopped. Took him to the hospital.

6:03 p.m. "Shooting" - Turned out to be a fight only, no shooting. No injury. LAPD handled.

7:05 p.m. "Injury" -15-year-old girl. Got a little 'crazy glue' in her eye. Her eye was slightly red, seemed all right. Flushed with water, advised mom to take her to the emergency room.

8:44 p.m. "Traffic" - Second Rescue to a multiple injury traffic accident. We handled a 25-year-old man who hit his throat on the steering wheel, and a 20-year-old woman who had a pain in her right side. They both looked fine but it had been a good crash, they were both placed on backboards with cervical collars and transported.

10:30 p.m. "ADW" - (Assault with a deadly weapon) A 45-year-old man beat with a gun during a robbery. Small laceration on the right temporal area (side of head) and to his left supra orbital area (above his eye.) Alert and oriented. Bandaged the cuts and advised he see a doctor, he wouldn't go with us.

11:06 p.m. "Sick" - 29-year-old man. Right lower abdominal pain all day. Said he has a history of an infected appendix. Started an IV, transported.

4:42 a.m. "Chest pain" - A 50-year-old man with chest and abdominal pain. IV, Nitroglycerin, transport.

DAY TWO

8:08 a.m. "Difficult respirations" - A 50-year-old woman with bilateral rales (fluid in both lungs) history of same. PAC's (premature atrial contractions; an abnormal, but not particularly dangerous Electrocardiogram finding.) IV, Lasix (a diuretic, causes the body to excrete fluid) transport.

11:16 a.m. "Auto ped" - (Automobile hit pedestrian). A six-year-old boy, ran out in the street to get a ball, he was in bad shape. Compound (open) fracture of the femur (thigh bone protruding out of the skin) rigid abdomen (a sign of internal bleeding). Backboard, cervical collar, Code 3 transport to hospital.

5:17 p.m. "Seizure" - False call, no patient there.

6:05 p.m. "Traffic" - Two patients. A 35-year-old female with a two-inch laceration on her arm and a one-inch laceration on her knee. A 34-year-old male with vertex (top of head) pain. Broke the windshield with his head, not wearing a seat belt. The man was placed on a back board with a cervical collar, the woman's cuts were bandaged, and both were transported to the hospital.

7:15 p.m. "Traffic" - No injuries, not needed.

8:10 p.m. "Difficult respirations" - Returned by radio (cancelled in route).

8:25 p.m. "Attempted suicide" - An elderly, senile man, drunk only. Left with family.

8:45 p.m. "Attempted suicide" - False, no such address.

9:09 p.m. "Injury" - 30-year-old man with pain in his left thigh and hip. Has past injury requiring pins in his femur. Transported.

10:27 p.m. "Man down" - Crazy transient. Wants a ride to the liquor store. Didn't get it.

10:38 p.m. "Shooting" - False call. No shooting at location.

4:44 a.m. "Assault" - Mental patient with nonspecific complaints of being 'sick'. Advised to private doctor, family will handle.

DAY THREE

9:34 a.m. "Injury" - A 25-year-old man, in jail. Small laceration on finger. Band-Aid.

10:30 a.m. "Injury" - 38-year-old female at a gas station pay phone, complaining of a sore knee. Advised she see a doctor.

12:41 p.m. "Sick" - 48-year-old woman. Drunk, uncooperative, says she doesn't want any help. Called police to get her off sidewalk.

2:05 p.m. "Injury" – 19-year-old male. Diving for a football in front yard. Hit his side on the curb. Complaining of pain with extreme point tenderness (pain to the touch) in left low back (kidney area.) Had to convince him to go with us. IV, transport. Had blood in urine at hospital (possible ruptured kidney).

3:24 p.m. "Injury" - Returned by radio in route to call.

4:29 p.m. "GSW" - (Gunshot wound) 22-year-old male. Shot in right upper quadrant of abdomen. Low blood pressure. IV, MAST suit, Code 3 to hospital.

6:25 p.m. "Shooting" - Family dispute only. Handled by LAPD.

6:31 p.m. "Woman down" - Hysterical due to family problems, no medical emergency.

8:10 p.m. "Overdose" - Refused help.

8:49 p.m. "Traffic" - Eight month pregnant 21-year-old. Slight abdominal pain. Transport.

9:27 p.m. "Structure fire" - 70-year-old female with second degree burns to face, chest, hands. Confused, uncooperative. Code 3 transport.

10:27 p.m. "Injury" - 30-year-old man, hit window with hand. Cut radial artery (on wrist.) Patient applied direct pressure to wound and had bleeding stopped by the time we arrived. Bandage and transport.

1:15 a.m. "Injury" - 40-year-old man complaining of being beat up six months ago and got a black eye. No new complaint. No treatment.

1:28 a.m. "Injury" - 50-year-old woman. Small cut on toe. No emergency.

2:12 a.m. "Person down" - 80-year-old female, fell out of bed. No injury, no complaints. Helped back to bed only.

2:44 a.m. "Traffic" - False, no traffic accident at the address.

6:09 a.m. "Seizure" -13-year-old male. History of frequent seizures. Confused. Transport.

Well that was it, and it turned out to be fairly typical. Thirty-nine calls in 72 hours; an average of 13 calls a day. Only one call after midnight each of the first two shifts and *five* after midnight the last shift. I *did* go home feeling like a zombie, as expected.

My wife did ask how it went. I rested on the couch while she read the blow by blow.

There were only 7 of the 39 calls which were 'serious' and required our immediate intervention. This is a good example for EMT's that most of what happens out there are EMT level calls, *not* Paramedic calls. I mention that because EMT's often feel less important than Paramedics, they aren't.

If I hadn't kept track of the calls, these three typically uneventful shifts would have been quickly and typically forgotten. Like most of them.

Chapter Forty-Three
Tired

*P*latoon duty they call it, it's 24 hour shifts.

Different departments vary in how they've chosen to set up their particular schedules; in L.A. it's like this, work-off-work-off-work-off-off-off-off-Repeat. . .

So we know for up to two years in advance what days we'll be working. It helps to prepare mentally, and to plan ahead for missing Christmas, or Thanksgiving, etc. There are three different shifts. The A, B, and C shifts. Isn't that cute. Each shift has its own color on a special calendar. The 'A' is red, 'B' is blue, and 'C' is green. Sounds almost like working on *Sesame Street* doesn't it? When time comes to put in transfer requests (every two years) you list your requests, and based on total time on the department, time in your particular rank, and the point value of your current assignment, you compete for the desirable assignments. Or, the method can vary with whatever transfer plan a particular Department comes up with.

I had been at a relatively desirable spot for two years (not worth many assignment points) so I got the 79th pick on my wish list of assignments. It could be worse, but it was bad enough. I could look forward to coming home tired after *every* shift for the next two years.

Fast forward. I'd been at my new assignment for almost two years, looking forward to going somewhere nicer in January. I hadn't been disappointed; I had gone home tired after *every* shift for almost two years; tonight, was no exception.

It was 3 a.m., our fourth call after midnight, eighteen so far this shift. I knew I should leave the Journal for the morning but that would mean I'd have to stay longer, and I wanted to get home.

Every call had to be recorded in the *Journal*. The time, address, type of call, name of the patient, the patient's vital signs and their complaint, what treatment we provided, where and when we transported if we did, what time we finished the call, the time we returned to the fire station, along with any other notable facts concerning the shift. I was entering the 18th call of the day. I was *really* tired. My eyelids were feeling pretty heavy. The fire station was dark and quiet and everyone else was sleeping, except me. I felt as if I should just lay my face in that book and let them find me there in the morning. I would have done it too, but I was afraid I'd drool on my entries. The Journal is a legal document, subject to being subpoenaed in court, they don't like drool on such things.

I could see the pen and my hand moving, and I knew what I wanted to write, and I swear I could see the words I was writing, and they looked like *regular* words. But, when my head dropped eight inches suddenly, and I startled awake, I noticed that the last ten words on the paper looked like something from the Dead Sea scrolls. It was gibberish, scribbles, squiggles, chicken scratches, a *Paper-Mate* gone mad. I had at least a line or two of these unintelligible wiggly worm entries each night.

The scary part is that I was *that* tired, and was out there making life and death decisions, and my partner was probably equally tired, and driving the ambulance. Yikes. There were plenty of late nights and early mornings when I was afraid I would fall asleep right there in the patient's living room, and suddenly fall flat on my face in the middle of their floor. Scary.

Chapter Forty-Four
"Don't trust anybody"

He smoked fat cigars, and had a body reflecting almost twenty years of late night snacks and fast food dinners.

He had a thousand stories, and was full of good advice for his brand new partner. *"The Fire Department is out to screw you kid, they're nothing but a bunch of disease ridden scum."* That was one of his more subdued remarks. He definitely had some strong views. His initials were **A.J.** and that's what everybody called him.

His rookie partner was proud he was a Paramedic, so was his girlfriend. It was just last week, graduation day, after the ceremony and the pinning on of his Paramedic certification pin, that his girlfriend handed him a gold-plated pen with his name engraved on it, along with a kiss to go with it.

His first shift as a Paramedic. They were driving a loop to all the area hospitals to become familiar with the parking areas, supply restocking procedures, and with the E.R. staff. As they merged with the traffic on the Hollywood freeway A.J. said, "Nice pen." You couldn't help but notice it, glowing there against the bright white shirt background.

He explained the pen's history, he was *proud* to be a Paramedic. A.J. took a couple of slow puffs on his cigar and said gruffly, "L'me see it."

The rookie quickly complied and handed the shiny prize over to A.J. He looked it over, inspecting it, and said, "That's nice" and then with a flip of his wrist, tossed it out the open window onto the freeway.

"Hey!"

"What?" A.J. said calmly.

"Why did you do that? Jesus!"

"Kid" he said. "On this job, don't trust anybody." That was A.J.

Chapter Forty-Five
Rat Patrol

Downtown L.A.

A beautiful City, it isn't. Most big cities share a common thread which runs through its fabric, a thread tattered and weathered, binding the tapestry which encompasses the bright and the beautiful, with the dark alleys and back streets.

Stories of big ol' brown rats in tenement houses, their bright red eyes glowing in the shadows, seemed a literary exaggeration, until I became a Paramedic. How else do you get a middle-class Caucasian to walk in the shadows of a darkened downtown midnight alley?

Paramedics walk in the Bel Air mansions of the famous, and in the putrid ooze of a dumpster dinner table.

I had a new partner. When I told him we were going on "Rat Patrol" that evening he said, "O.K., what's that?"

"Just get us downtown around 6th and Wall about midnight."

"O.K." he said.

It was 1 a.m. We had just transported to USC. I'd forgotten about the 'Rat Patrol' promise until we passed 7th and Wall.

"We're here" my partner announced. "What about Rat Patrol?"

That woke me up. "Turn right."

"Here?"

"Right there! The alley. Turn the headlights off." We bounced into the black alley. "Stop!" There we sat.

My partner looked over at me. "So, what's the Rat Patrol?"

"That's *us*" I said. See the dumpster up there on the right? Not this one, the next one, up there."

"Yeah."

"When I tell you to, drive up to it fast and stop pointing right toward it, then switch on your high beams, quick."

He sat there poised at the wheel.

"Now!" The wheels squealed and spun, we lurched forward and slid to a stop five feet from the dumpster. When the headlights burst on no less than 10 huge brown rats froze momentarily, stared us in the eyes, and then bounded off in every direction

"All right! That's great!" hollered my partner. Just then a disturbance behind the huge can caught our eyes. Up popped two filthy vermin.

"What's going on" the men called out, eyes wide with fear.

I rolled down my window. "Just the Rat Patrol, it's O.K." I answered.

"Oh, uh, all right" one man said. They both looked at each other and shook their heads approvingly.

It's like Jacques Cousteau said, "There's another world out there. It covers most of the Earth and yet is as foreign to most men as is the surface of the Moon." He was talking about the ocean, but there's another world out there, and most of us are oblivious to it.

Chapter Forty-Six
"Drop the gun!"

We'd just pulled up in front of the apartment building; the call was to an "Injury." A police car was down the street heading slowly toward us, its spotlight was hopping from one address to the next.

I had the 'Red book' under my left arm, my partner came around the front of the Rescue carrying the White box, together we started toward the building. We'd only gone a few steps when I saw a man wobbling down a stairway across the driveway in front of us. "He's got a gun, get back to the Rescue" I told my partner.

The police car had stopped twenty feet in front of us on the other side of the driveway. I was standing near the passenger door of the Rescue, the Policemen had just left their car, the man was at the base of the stairs and turned toward us, the gun was in his right hand pointing down, "Put the gun down!" I called out.

The police officers quickly drew their guns and turned toward the man. "Don't move! Police!" The man looked up and continued to stagger down the driveway toward the officers. The police shouted in Spanish to drop the gun and don't move. The officers were crouched in a combat stance, their guns trained on the man. The man was less than fifteen feet away. My partner and I had moved to the rear of the ambulance for cover. I was sure the police would fire any moment. The man continued toward them, gun at his side, less than ten feet away. The officers continued to shout commands at the man. One of the policemen moved to the right circling behind him.

From behind, the officer reached quickly for the gun, pulled it from the man's hand, then pushed the man to the ground.

He was just drunk. I don't know why he had the gun, but apparently, he had no intention of using it. The officers would certainly have been justified in shooting the man as he waved that gun up and down, sometimes pointing it right at them. They could have shot him; I think I would have.

I'd seen plenty of examples of restraint by the police, but this one really impressed me. When they hand cuffed the man and sat him in the back seat of their car, I realized we could just have easily been covering him with a sheet.

It's an awesome responsibility, to give someone a gun and send them out day after day to enforce the law and protect the citizenry.

It's a tough job and getting tougher, but they do a damn good job.

Chapter Forty-Seven
Teacher

He was my teacher in Paramedic school. He showed me how to hook the L.A.F.D belt buckle on my belt.

I looked up to him. I believed in him. I took his advice and made it a part of my beliefs as a Paramedic.

He'd been a Police officer with the L.A.P.D for a few years, before coming over to the fire department and training as a Paramedic. He said he reviewed the entire library of Paramedic training manuals every year to stay sharp, and to be the best Paramedic he could be; it's a stack of five *fat* manuals.

I saw him around midnight in the back of his ambulance in the parking lot of *California* hospital. It was two days before he killed himself. He seemed just like his old self, said he was doing fine, made a little joke about something and said they were getting beat up all night, and that he was tired.

In the years since then I've heard a half dozen stories about troubles in his life, and reasons why he did it. None of the stories explained it to me, of course how could they.

Being a Paramedic he'd seen hundreds of suicides and suicide attempts. If there's a group who could be counted on to put on a successful suicide, it's Paramedics.

He was studying for *Supervisor*, and it seemed like he was looking to the future. He went to meet an old friend to talk over the supervisor test. When his friend wasn't there he left a note for him, and told him where he was.

He parked his car across the street, put a coat hanger around his neck, hooked it to the rear-view mirror, and then shot himself in the forehead with a hollow point .38 bullet. In case, as often occurs, he continued reflex breathing (controlled by the primitive portion of the brain at the brain stem) the clothes hanger noose would cut off air and circulation when he slumped forward.

By the time his buddy came back to the station, found the note, and made it over to the car, it was over. He'd learned so much in sixteen years as a Paramedic. He'd been a student of death, and submitted his doctorate thesis that afternoon.

Chapter Forty-Eight
It's loaded

Guns are dangerous, that's obvious enough; well you'd *think* it was obvious enough.

Before handling any gun, you need to be trained. There's no room for mistakes when you're handling a deadly weapon. Police officers undergo exhaustive training in the use of their weapons, as well as regular retraining and frequent qualifying practice. I guess if I were to pick a group of weapons handling experts, other than soldiers, it would be police officers.

I'll bet it's just coincidence, that I happened to handle personally *all* of the accidental shootings involving police officers. I've been on *three* of them. There *couldn't* have been *more* than that.

One Sheriff took out his new model 60 Smith & Wesson to show a fellow officer his new grips, and shot himself in the thigh. An LAPD officer wounded himself while showing off *his* new gun and holster. Luckily none of those accidental shootings was serious. They were more damaging to their pride than to their anatomy.

Now the third one was different, and the officer involved was more stupid than the others. I can say that, *stupid* fits in this case. He was working part-time on his off days as a security officer in a nightclub on Pico Boulevard in L.A. He knew the lady who owned the place, and worked there as a favor and a change of pace.

He was upstairs in the office with the owner and a few friends. The owner asked to see his gun. He took it from his waistband holster and handed it to her. She promptly pointed it at his stomach, smiled, and pulled the trigger. She said later she didn't think it would be loaded. Well at least the officer wasn't the *only* stupid person involved in the shooting; it's nice to interact with your peers.

We were notified by the dispatcher that the patient was an off-duty LAPD officer. We were close by, just clearing a call from California Hospital.

My partner and I bounded up the outside stairway to the office. One look at him and we both knew instantly he was in *big* trouble. He was flat on his back, holding his abdomen. He was cold, clammy, and pale as a sheet. He was awake, talking to us softly. He figured he would die, he said so.

We had the MAST suit inflated and two 14-gauge IV's going in less than five minutes. I told him to "Hang in there" and that "We're going to do everything we can for you."

I didn't think he would live, we couldn't even palpate a blood pressure. He was at the hospital two minutes later.

It was almost two years later. I'd transferred out of downtown and was working in Venice near the beach. The call over the PA said, "Hodge, visitor in quarters!" I wondered who it could be, I didn't get many visitors at work.

The man in the office looked slightly familiar but I couldn't place him. He held a bottle of wine in his left hand and held his right hand out to me.

"Do you remember me?" he asked.

"Well you look familiar" I said, uncomfortable at not remembering.

"It's been a while. I've been trying to track you down. You changed stations." He told me his name and said he was the policeman who got shot in the bar on Pico.

"Oh yeah, I remember *that*" I said shaking my head. He told me about the operation and the six months to recover, and went on about how I'd saved his life.

He thanked me, and I told him I was glad he did O.K. He smiled, shook my hand again, handed me the wine, and said one final "Thank you."

"You're welcome" I said.

I don't like wine, and we weren't allowed to have alcohol at the station. So, I gave the bottle to the Captain, he also said, "Thank you."

Chapter Forty-Nine
"Stick em up!"

They parked out front, across from the bank. The driver handed the other man a gun.

It would be easy, give the teller a note. "Empty all your cash into a large deposit bag, don't set off the alarm or you're dead."

The teller nervously filled the bag and handed it to the man. The security guard had picked up on the fidgeting man at window three. He un-clipped his holster and put his hand on the butt of his old 38. As the man took the bag and turned to leave, the teller dropped behind the counter to the floor and hit the alarm. The guard spun to confront the man, "Freeze!" They fired together. Behind the security guard a child fell wounded. The money bag almost fell as a bullet tore into the man's shoulder. Another shot, the robber groaned and grabbed his chest. He was almost to the door, suddenly the glass door shattered around him, he turned and fired twice, a woman dropped, the guard fell to one knee, with a bullet in his leg. The guard fired again, twice. A bullet ripped through the man's back and out his chest, another cut through his right hand and the bag of money fell. The would-be robber stumbled and fell on the sidewalk just outside the bank.

It was a classic call. The robber lay mortally wounded outside the bank; the security guard was holding a handkerchief on his leg and answering questions for the LAPD officers. Two people in the bank had minor wounds.

We crunched through the window glass and knelt next to the wounded man. He was groaning. He looked up at me and asked if he was going to die. I thought he would. "Just hold still and we'll do what we can" I told him.

We were in route to Daniel Freeman hospital in a few minutes. We squeezed the IV bags as the policeman riding with us asked the man questions. I lifted the oxygen mask off his face as he answered.

"I owed him money. He said this would make us even. Man, I made a mistake."

The policeman seemed to have asked all the important questions, but I chimed in.

"How much did you owe him?" I asked.

"$270. I bought my mom stuff for her house. Don't let me die. Oh God!"

He was awake and alert but I couldn't get any peripheral pulses. He was going to die.

I wondered if his story was true, it was so ridiculous I figured it was. He begged us to save his life, and we tried, but his mistake was too big, and we couldn't fix it.

Chapter Fifty
A day off

Seems like many of us involved in EMS become involved in other forms of helping people outside of our regular job.

You'd think we'd get enough at work, apparently not. I know dozens of L.A. City Paramedics or Firefighters who work part time as members of ski patrol teams, or mountain search and rescue teams, or as reserve police officers and Sheriff's deputies, nurses, CPR instructors, EMT instructors, etc.

I wanted to find out where the bad guys hung out in my town. I wanted to know where the dealers were selling and where the robberies and assaults were going down. I wanted to know my community's dark side and use this knowledge to keep my wife and kids away from it. It wasn't strictly selfish when I became a Reserve Sheriff's Deputy, I truly wanted to help in my community. I was worried about the skyrocketing population in my sleepy little town, and the resulting increase in crime of all sorts. I wanted to help keep it safe. After six months of training, every Monday evening and all day every Sunday, I was sworn in as a Level 1, L.A. County Sheriff's Deputy Reserve.

I found it difficult to devote the time necessary to complete the extensive field training program, and later switched from street patrol to the *Sheriff's Mountain Search and Rescue Team*, which required less time commitment. I enjoyed the training in search techniques, rappelling, steep angle rescue, etc. but didn't have the same reaction and motivation as the other team members. After all, I'd been out there on the streets of L.A. for years handling thousands and thousands of emergency rescue calls. The other guys, who worked as realtors, engineers, telephone installers, shop owners, etc. thought it was really exciting to get called out in the middle of the night for a lost child, tramp around in the mountains for six hours, only to find out the kid had been over at a friend's house, then get home at 3 a.m. and get up for work at 5 a.m. It may have been exciting for *them*; it was just another 'false call' for me.

It was 8:30 p.m. on a cold and gloomy January. The phone rang. It was Ed Green, the Captain of the search and rescue team. "We've got a 12-year-old boy lost at Mountain High (a nearby ski area.) It's snowing heavily up there right now, can you make it?" I looked over at my wife, we had just gotten home from visiting my mom, and we were both dead tired and had plans for tomorrow. I grimaced as I replied.

"Yeah, I'll go. Gonna meet at the station?"

He said yes.

"O.K. I'll be there in 15 minutes." I wasn't thrilled.

I pulled on my long underwear, grabbed my pack from the garage, tied my crampons and ice axe onto the pack, kissed my wife and headed out.

An hour and a half later I was in snow shoes trudging up a steep mountain in a driving snow storm.

The boy had left his group heading to the parking lot, he told them he was getting cold. The church group of teenagers had planned the snow trip on the spur of the moment, and they weren't properly dressed.

It wasn't unusual to find the snow play areas full of people in tennis shoes and short sleeve shirts. The nearby towns could be basking in 80 degree temperatures, while 30 minutes up the mountain, in deep snow, the wind-chill could cause daytime temperatures to plummet into the teens.

The youngster had last been seen heading to the parking lot, it was only a few hundred feet away, over a little rise. The snow was beginning to fall heavily. Considering the way he was dressed, he was probably suffering one of the early effects of hypothermia, *confusion*, when he headed to the parking area but went the wrong direction.

I hoped he'd gone home in another car and that somehow the group leader had made a mistake. I hoped he was at some friend's house now. I hoped this would be another false call. But I had a bad feeling. We were searching behind every tree, log, boulder, and bush. The snow had been falling heavily for hours. It was cold and getting colder fast. If he was out there he'd been exposed to frigid temperatures and heavy snow for over five hours now. I thought at this point it had become a body search. I hoped I was wrong. I began to move faster as I searched. I wanted to find him, and yet, I didn't.

It was 3 a.m. We'd gone back to the base and entered our search on the map. We were updated on the areas searched by other teams. We downed cups of hot chocolate or coffee, and had a couple of donuts before heading back out

We found a lone set of tracks, tracks almost covered over by the driving snow. The group gathered up to comb the area. The tracks headed up a hill, past a locked outhouse, up to a ridge. On the ridge the tracks faded. The snow was blowing hard horizontally, visibility was less than 20 feet and the temperature was brutal.

From the ridge, between the flurries, tiny patches of light below marked the city of Palmdale. From here it seemed almost close, but it was some 20 miles away, down steep icy chutes and impassable canyons; it was a fatal goal for anyone to attempt.

The victim of hypothermia becomes confused, and often does things which to them may seem reasonable, and which may prove deadly.

The tracks were gone. We searched every bush and rock and lump in the snow. If they were his tracks, he had ended up at the worst possible part of the mountain, at the worst possible time. The snow bit hard and stung our faces as we searched through blizzard conditions.

It was almost sunrise; other teams had arrived to replace us. We reported the location of the tracks and hiked up to the command post. I was beat.

It was around 10 a.m. when one of the teams found him. He was on the ridge, where we had found the tracks.

I knew one of the guys on the Malibu team, he was also a City Paramedic. He was the one who found him, mostly buried by the snow; a tuft of hair was all they saw at first. He was basically frozen, but they worked him up anyway. They air lifted him out and continued to attempt rewarming and resuscitation at the hospital. After an extensive effort, he was pronounced dead.

My work on the Sheriff's Search and Rescue Team was largely relaxing, a change of pace, something *fun*. But not this time. The team that found him said he was found just 15 or 20 feet from our snow shoe tracks. We'd been right there. We missed him.

I realized of course that it wasn't our fault, we did a good search. We just didn't go quite far enough. You can't cover every inch of the mountain. He was most likely dead by then anyway. I knew all that.

I wrote this a month later:

Somewhere in a snowflake
I am so cold, where have the others gone?
I feel so far away and yet I know you wait just there,
I see my tracks in front of me, round the trees,
a snowy dream this has to be,
I don't belong here, not alone, where have the others gone?
I'm sure my path was true. Jump out now, from behind the trees and
bushes weighted down white, circle around laughing, point at me.
How silly I must look puffing my steamy breaths, hugging myself,
put your arms around me, warm me with your laughter,
pat me on the back.
I'm smiling with eyes closed, I thought I heard you there, somewhere in a
snowflake driven hard,
and how strange it is now,
on this ridge where lights below are another world,
and only moments ago my cheek was stung by every missile in quiet fury,
but now, no longer need I escape, with eyes closed I cannot tell who has laid
it upon me but I feel it warm on my back.

In some snowy dream I guess, and I smile, seeing myself,
how silly I must look nestled warm as I am and all of
them around me puffing steamy breaths in the morning sun,
this must be some silly dream,
somewhere in a snowflake.

Chapter Fifty-One
Mom

She was a transient, a street person, and crazy to boot. Unfortunately, she was also a new mom.

It was about 6 a.m. We were called to an alley behind a dormitory at USC. She was sitting there in the front seat of someone's station wagon. She'd delivered her baby there a few hours earlier.

It only took a few moments of questioning to conclude she wasn't *all there*. I wanted to get the baby away from her, I didn't trust her. She didn't have the baby covered, and it was a cool morning. She had pierced the newborn's left ear with a bobby pin. She was feeding herself and the baby mustard from a fast food mustard packet which she had smeared onto an air conditioning vent on the dash. Whenever I asked her to let me look at the baby, she squeezed him tightly and refused.

My partner went to the ambulance and called for the P.D. We told dispatch to have them standby around the comer; I didn't want to provoke her.

I continued trying to convince her that she would have to let us examine the baby. She wasn't going for it. I tried everything I could think of; saying we had to take his temperature, we needed to check his blood pressure, we want to give him some milk. She almost went for "We have to weigh him."

She was acting more and more irrational, and wasn't making much sense at all. She definitely had bats in her belfry, or a bad case of postpartum depression. Finally, looking her straight in the eye, and saying it sternly, I said, "O.K. If you don't want our help were leaving, but I have to get the baby's foot print on the birth certificate, it's a State law. We don't have any choice. It'll take one minute, and then we'll leave." She looked at me about to say something, then, handed the baby to me. My partner picked up the cold placenta which was laying on the ground just outside the car door, and followed me to the rear of the car, where he quickly clamped and cut the umbilical cord.

My partner waved to the police who were waiting and watching just around the corner. The mom sat there calmly, and never looked toward us or mentioned the baby again. The police handcuffed her and began to question her about the infant.

"I never had a baby" she said. She began a rambling filibuster about taxes and Ronald Reagan and the FBI.

I truly believe she had no idea what had happened, and that to her the baby, and us, and the police, and Ronald Reagan, all just sort of blended together, and faded in and out, and became a jumbled part of her broken world.

I wondered what would become of the baby, and if one day he would try to find out about his 'real mom', and hoped he wouldn't.

Chapter Fifty-Two
The Coroner's office

Shock value, it's definitely that!

The class was scheduled for a tour at 9 a.m. Most of us were looking forward to it, sort of. I think more than anything else it's an attempt to desensitize us, and perhaps weed out some of these would-be paramedics.

The Coroner's office. It was an old building, located just down the street from County hospital. The class of 30 shuffled quietly in, past the old glass double doors and down a short hallway past the antique elevator. Single file we entered the glossy pale green metal staircase, clanking down two flights to the basement.

At the first landing a low moan began. Like the 'wave' in the stands at a Friday night football game, it flowed through the 30 *green* paramedic trainees. As the air thickened, the faces of several of my classmates suddenly disappeared, as they transformed and blended into the pale green stairs and walls around us.

As the door was flung open in front of us, the odor of death encased us, weighed us down. I wanted to leave. I looked behind me to the door as it clicked closed. The exit sign flickered above the door, dying, its last flashes like the final heartbeat of some poor, stiff, cold, smelly soul, shuffled from the refrigerator to the stainless steel table in front of me.

The Deputy Coroners enjoy these tours. It gives them a chance to show that their line of work hasn't dampened their sense of humor.

We gathered in a half circle around the table, as the coroner uncovered the body of a young black man. The doctor displayed the depth of the stab wounds by placing a tongue depressor in each hole. It was bad enough, I thought, to shove a dozen popsicle sticks in this fellow, but then the white coated PhD., who I thought was really Freddie Kruger beneath that coat, grabbed a scalpel from the instrument tray and slit Jerome from just below his ribs to right above his private parts, well, *formerly* private. Out came long wiggly coils of slimy intestines, squishing out like some primeval anatomical eruption.

The odor from Jerome's interior mixed with, then covered over, the previous atmosphere. It was no longer just a sickening stench it was a *taste* now. I really wanted to vomit but the thought of puking there, all over my classmates, or perhaps right there on Jerome's liver, was just too disgusting to consider. So, I just stood there, semiconscious, pale, weak, diaphoretic, dazed, and stuporous, thinking it could get no worse.

Then he grabbed the skull saw. No not Jerome, the doctor. Although in my present state I'd swear Jerome had made a move for it. The saw chewed into the skull from the forehead horizontally around to the back, in a strange primitive "bowl cut' from a deranged barber.

Oh yeah, I guess I blocked out this part. Before the saw and popping the lid off of Jerome's skull, the skin at the back of the head had to be cut then pulled up and over in a big flap across Jerome's face. This technique was perfected by the Apache Indians, and must be accompanied by a loud whooping call. We all stood there, eyes wide, jaws hanging open until the coroner completed the ritual. The work of the skull saw would be hidden when Jerome's face was pulled back in place. If the family wanted an open casket Jerome would look nice. I guess they removed the Popsicle sticks too.

To make a nauseating story short, Jerome's brain was removed and sliced up along with all the other major organs for samples to determine exactly which of the dozen or so stab wounds had killed him, and if any other factors were involved. When Dr. Frankenstein had finished, Jerome looked like a hollowed-out canoe, with his rib cage split down the middle and spread open exposing an empty frame of bone, cartilage, and pink tissue. Jerome's parts, his brain, heart, lungs, kidneys, stomach, intestines, spleen, diaphragm, and other assorted bits and pieces, were all sloshing about in a big five gallon plastic bucket. Jerome lay there on the table looking like the table scraps after a feline meal on the Serengeti.

I was getting into this a little by this time. I think the lack of oxygen or the smell of formaldehyde was to blame, but I did laugh hysterically for some reason when the coroner joked about skinning Jerome and making a wet suit out of him. Jerome was black, so the remark was far from politically correct, maybe the formaldehyde was to blame.

The bucket of parts was dumped back into Jerome's chest, and a fat needle with thick thread quickly mended the gaping cavern.

The tour continued for a while. Nobody fainted, and yes, I guess we were desensitized a bit that day. Maybe it was a good thing, maybe the sooner you get used to death the better off you'll be in this job.

The coroner took a bite of his ham sandwich as he said good-bye to us. A bit of crust fell and landed right in the middle of Jerome's open left eye. I winced a little for Jerome, it's the least I could do.

Chapter Fifty-Three
Victor

I'd learned about it through the rumor mill. A fellow paramedic, a classmate, a friend, had *Aids*.

At first the rumors said no, it was an intestinal disease. That's why he was getting so thin, but not Aids.

As the rumors turned to fact, I began to feel the vulnerability, for me, for all paramedics. We were exposed all right, even though a few years ago our department began to *require* the use of latex gloves, we were still at risk. The gloves often tore, sometimes just by putting them on, low bidder I think. There were many times when we would be working on someone for ten or fifteen minutes, only to find a rip in the fingertip of our glove, and our hand covered in blood beneath the glove.

Our patients cough on us, spit at us, vomit, and even have the nerve to bleed all over us. Everybody in the business appreciates the risk of communicable diseases. We're taught how to minimize the risk of exposure, but for too many of us the routine nature of our exposure to disease translates into a routinely lax application of what we've learned. For a while it seemed to me that many paramedics had adopted the macho stupidity they'd learned from their firefighter compatriots. Firefighters in the L.A.F.D had a tough time trading in their "Fireman" badges for "Firefighter" badges when the name change decree came down. They were 'men' damn it, and God help the women 'Firemen' who had turned them into mere 'Firefighters.'

In the old days, the firemen would avoid using 'breathers' (self-contained breathing apparatus.) They would suck in clouds of toxic smoke, and seemed to like it. They'd cough and choke and spit out black soot tinged phlegm while joking about the near collapse of a charred roof. Times changed. The firefighters started using breathers. The paramedics started to use latex gloves, and everybody grew up a bit. Of course, the poisons of exposure didn't appreciate this learning curve. For many firefighters, the cancers would punctuate their lapse and become the terror of their retirement. For many paramedics, the Aids virus may be waiting, waiting to transform us into the wasting, pitiful, patients we dreaded.

In Victor, the worst case had occurred. He only had a couple of months to live. The fire department labeled his illness non-duty related and refused to pay for his disability. It made sense for the City, at least financially, and maybe they knew some of Victor's secrets, either way it was sad and I just hated to know he was dying.

Someday they'll be a cure for Aids. Someday everybody may be able to turn their fear to compassion. Someday, maybe, a time will come when someone like Victor can die content and in peace. But for now, people like Victor must break new ground, and live their final days in turmoil, struggling to maintain some dignity in a world that gives them little.

He wasn't a movie star, he was no Magic Johnson. But he was my friend, and I miss him.

Note: Since then things *have* changed. People with Aids don't become a social pariah to most, and advances in medicine have transformed some with HIV, *essentially* curing them.

Chapter Fifty-Four
"He'll be fine"

After completing the classroom phase of the paramedic training program, the perspective paramedics must undergo a minimum of (20) 24-hour shifts under the observation and guidance of a certified two-person paramedic crew.

The paramedic trainee must demonstrate the ability to turn his book knowledge into actual field patient care. It's always interesting to watch a trainee develop in the relatively short period of twenty shifts. The seasoned paramedics make sure that the basics of *street survival* are instilled in the new paramedic, to help the trainee avoid a stupid mistake which could get somebody hurt or killed.

Developing appropriate bedside manner takes a while for most of them. It's always a good idea to stick to the facts, and not to mislead the patient or family regarding the patient's condition. It's much easier to accept a bad outcome if you see it coming.

This was our trainee's first shift. We'd been talking for about an hour when we got the call to a 50-year-old male with chest pain. On the way to the call we were going over possible scenarios, and drilling our trainee on the various treatments possible, depending on the evaluation of the patient.

We were met in front of the house by the patient's wife, who was very upset. She told us he had just gotten up this morning when he suddenly threw up and said he had a terrible pain in his chest. As we entered the living room we could hear him moaning. Our trainee was in front of us with the defibrillator and the drug box. He'd been told to take charge of the call.

"Sir we're the paramedics, we need to ask some questions, and my partner is going to place some oxygen under your nose." The trainee was doing pretty good. He was smooth and confident. My partner slipped the 02 cannula around the patient's head while I began to enter patient information on our form. We already knew he was 57 years old from his wife, and that he had no previous medical problems, and took no medications.

"Pulse is about 60 and irregular" the trainee said after palpating the radial pulse. "Let's hook up the scope" he said. I looked up at my partner, his eyebrows were raised up and he flashed a little smirk. We were impressed, so far. I attached the electrode patches to the man's chest as the trainee continued his questioning. "Sir does your pain travel anywhere else, or is it just in the center of your chest where you're touching."

"No it goes down into my left arm too" he said.

"What does the pain feel like? How would you describe it?"

"It's heavy like a weight pressing down on me."

"Sinus Brady at 56, with ten to twelve unifocal PVC's a minute" my partner announced.

"O.K. set up a normal saline with a mini drip." The trainee ordered. "On a scale of one to ten, with ten being the worst pain you've ever had, what number is the pain you have now?"

"It's ten" the man said, looking pale and becoming increasingly diaphoretic.

"We need to start an IV in case we need to give you some medicines" I explained.

"O.K." he said to me weakly.

"What orders do you expect?" I asked, quizzing the trainee.

"Nitro, M.S., and Lidocaine, maybe Atropine" he answered quickly.

"O.K. call it in" I said.

It was a little unusual to put the trainee on the radio on his first shift, but I had a feeling he'd do fine.

"His B.P is 98 over 50, respirations 24 and clear" my partner announced.

The trainee switched on the Biocom while my partner and I taped the IV line in place.

"Brotman base, Rescue 43."
"This is Brotman, go ahead 43."
"We're at the home of an alert and oriented 57-year-old male, approximately 240 pounds, complaining of sub-sternal chest pain radiating to his left arm. He's had the pain for about one hour since getting out of bed this morning, and had one episode of vomiting just prior to this pain. He describes the pain as a heavy, crushing sensation. He rates this pain a ten on a scale of 1-10. We have him on 02 by nasal cannula at six liters. We see a sinus bradycardia of 56 with 10-12 multifocal PVC's per minute, up to this time we had only seen unifocal PVC's but now are seeing multifocal and an occasional back to back. The patient has no previous medical history, takes no medications, and has no allergies to medicine. We have a normal saline IV going TKO, our closest facility is you with a six-minute ETA, over."

My partner and I looked at each other and smiled, just a little smile so he wouldn't notice, he was good.

"Roger Rescue 43, give the patient one nitro spray 1/150 grain sublingual. Bolus the patient with 100 milligrams of Lidocaine. We're open and can accept the patient. If you could give us an updated BP after the nitro, and make sure he's supine I'd appreciate it, and what's your sequence number 43."

"Roger Brotman from 43, sequence number is C839146, copy one Nitro spray 1/150 sublingual and 100 milligrams of Lidocaine IV push. We'll get back to you in just a minute with an updated BP, we do have the patient supine and we will be transporting to your facility with a six-minute ETA after we get the patient down stairs from his second floor apartment."

Well, we gave the medications and the patient had relief of his pain, and his heart rate went up to 78; he looked pretty good.

As we left the house the man's 18-year-old daughter started to cry and said, "Don't let him die" to our trainee as we passed by.

The trainee reached out and put his hand on her shoulder and said, "Don't worry he'll be fine, he's not going to die."

I cringed a bit when I heard that and later gave the trainee a little talking to about it.

An hour after we left the hospital the man went into cardiac arrest and died.

Our trainee had a lot to learn after all. In this business, as in life, it's important not to make promises you can't keep.

Chapter Fifty-Five
Her father

The alarm pulsated with an inhuman undulating electronic squelch. I rolled over and slapped the snooze button on top of the beast and prayed for a power failure.

"Damn" I said, as I threw back the covers. I remembered the alarm had a battery backup, there was no stopping it. I smacked the red off button and stared blurry eyed at the time. The shining numbers burned into my consciousness in all their bright red neon glory proclaiming "4:15 a.m."

I was yawning when I first saw my reflection in the bathroom mirror. My hair was tweaked into an electric shock / Bozo hairdo. My eyes looked sunken and dark, squinting under the dual 100-watt glare. I stood there, eyes closed, hunched over the sink, and blindly smeared shaving cream over my face.

By 4:45 I was shaved, showered, and dressed. I looked more alive as I re-checked the image in the mirror, but *felt* the same.

It was 5 O'clock. I'd stopped at the *Yum-Yum* donut shop on the corner to make sure I started the day with a wholesome breakfast. I grabbed the little white bag containing my two chocolate donuts, snatched up the two milk containers, and broke a brief pre-sugar rush smile as I walked back to my car.

The freeway zipped along in the morning darkness. It wouldn't bog down for another 20 minutes. I was in front of the mess, like a skier in front of an avalanche.

6:15 a.m. I turned right on Hoover and right again into the driveway of Fire Station 46. It was the third and last day of my segment, after today I'd have four days off. I walked past the basketball hoop and opened the back door. The rescue and engine were in and the rookie from yesterday's shift was busy drying off the Chief's car that he'd already washed.

I headed up the stairs, then down the hall past the kitchen, and quietly into the RA room. The desk light was on and in the dim glow my partner was reading the entries of yesterday's runs. The 'A' shift paramedics were buried under their covers, lifeless mounds. I whispered to my partner "Do you think they're dead?" One of the corpses mumbled "Fuck you" and rolled over.

I grabbed the RA keys from the jumpsuit draped over the chair next to the nasty tongued corpse. My partner and I slipped out the door. What's that they say about a sleeping dog? Well these guys were dog tired and we hoped they'd reciprocate tomorrow morning.

"They had 19 calls, 7 after midnight" my partner said, shaking his head.

"Oh man" I sighed. The calls after midnight were above average, and we were used to statistics like that, 46's was a killer.

My partner and I had worked together for over a year. We knew each other's moves by now, we were a pretty good team.

I finished up a piece of toast with grape jelly and was reading the editorial section of the *Times*. My partner looked over at me from the sink where he was washing up a few of yesterday's dishes. (Actually, I'm giving him a little more credit than he's due. 46's has two dishwashers, and he was loading the dirty dishes into one of them.) He said in a subdued voice, "We're not out of service are we?" We hadn't had a call and it was 7:45.

"Shhhhh" I said, putting a finger to my lips. There's an unwritten rule that if you say something like that it will upset the Karma somehow and you'll get a run.

It should be a *written* rule I guess. The tone from the kitchen speaker snapped the morning calm. I looked at my partner and he looked at me, we didn't say a word but felt comforted in a strange way, somehow knowing there were powerful forces out there bigger than both of us, or the fire department.

"Engine 46 move emergency to fire station 37, OCD clear." My partner and I smiled together smugly.

"Super Bowl Sunday for the girls" I called to my partner. The "Girls" were the "Guys" and I guess the insult came partly from habit and partly from jealousy. The Firemen would generally have fewer calls during the shift, and usually their calls could be handled quicker. So while we were starting IV's, driving to a hospital, or calling a run in to the base station, they would be reclining, hands behind their heads, popcorn bowl on their laps, coke cans next to their seat, watching the football game.

"No, I sense a big structure fire" my partner predicted aloud.

"We'll see, maybe they'll..." The dispatch tone interrupted my next wisecrack.

"Rescue 46 to a shooting... standby 46... Rescue 46 pick up the Rescue phone." The Rescue phone was the beige one next to the toaster. The firemen had a red phone. I reminded myself to keep that thought. We should have a nice *blue* phone, I complained to myself.

"46" I said into the bland beige receiver.

"46 there's a shooting at 43nd place and Denker. The SWAT team is there and want you to standby. Go non-emergency and meet the PD there."

"Oky-doak" I snipped.

I repeated the message to my partner and we walked downstairs. There were poles for sliding from the upstairs to the downstairs, but this was a non-emergency call, so we'd walk the stairs.

I don't get too excited by the dispatch type or scenario. They usually turn out to be a lot less exciting than they sound. A "shooting" might end up to be a traffic accident or a sick person or even a false call. The dispatchers did their best, but you get some strange people calling 9-1-1, and sometimes you just can't decipher their message.

Three minutes later we were there. "This looks like the real deal" I said to my partner.

"What was your first clue" he snapped back smiling. The fifteen police cars, the SWAT van, and everyone running around with shotguns sort of gave it away.

I stepped out of my door in the direction of a plain clothes detective. My partner grabbed the trauma box and followed behind me. The detective had his walkie-talkie up close to his ear and glanced over at us approaching. "Hey, you guys got some business. SWAT found three D.B's and one live one."

Just then out of the front door of the house one of the SWAT guys came running. He was carrying a little girl, maybe 6-years-old; she looked dead, flopping like a doll in his arms. He ran straight to me, and handed her off like a baton in a relay race. I turned around and ran toward the rescue, trying as I ran to see where she was hurt. She was alive; I knew that as soon as I held her. She looked up at me, with painful, questioning eyes.

"Set up a saline, I'll get the MAST suit" I called to my partner as I laid her on the gurney. I pulled up her blood-soaked T-shirt with my left hand and simultaneously grabbed the MAST suit box with my right. "She's got an entrance just below the umbilicus, her abdomen's rigid."

"Lines ready" my partner said moments later, as he pumped up the blood pressure cuff. I had a 16-gauge IV started in her antecubital by the time I heard my partner again. "40 palp. Pulse is about 140, weak." We were both pulling the MAST suit around her legs and abdomen and attaching the Velcro closures. It was routine, we had to do the right things and do them quickly, the little girl was dying.

"Daniel Freeman 46" I said into the Biocom.
"Freeman, go 46."
"Are you open to trauma?"
"Roger 46."
"Let's go" I said to my partner who was already out of the ambulance with the side door half closed. I quickly gave the radio report while my partner drove a fast five-minute code 3 to the E.R. The little girl only moaned and looked at me with those wide and painful brown eyes. I told her the doctor would take care of her, and that she would be all right. I held her little hand in mine and could feel her trying to hold mine back.

I'm not sure if she lived. I asked at the E.R a week or so later but they weren't sure.

I never tried too hard to find out. I guess I didn't want to know. I wanted to believe she was fine, out riding her bicycle or roller skating with her friends, and that maybe somehow, she would just forget that day when her father had killed her mother and sister and brother, and had tried to kill her. I didn't want to believe that the little girl whose big brown eyes met mine that day would never see another birthday cake, and that the pain and hurt and horror of that day were her last memories.

I hope she's alive today, but I still hurt, for all the other little girls with big brown painful eyes.

Chapter Fifty-Six
Heroes

I'll be glad to be done with it. I don't want to be a hero.

Paramedics save lives every day, and often risk their own. They ruin their knees and backs and hearts.

The decomposing bodies, the tears of pain from the mothers, fathers, brothers and sisters, the circle of love around us all so easily shattered.

Trying so hard to heal the wounds, and being wounded in the process. The decisions, when to start or stop, and who can be 'salvaged'. When the sick jokes start to hurt, when the pain becomes yours.

I'll be glad to be done with it. I don't want to be a hero.

Chapter Fifty-Seven
Too much T.V.

It was January and Hollywood was chilly that night. The hookers were forced to bundle up a bit and to make their sidewalk displays short and sweet.

The LAPD had recently begun a nightly round up of prostitutes, which further impacted upon the ability of these *professionals* to ply their trade.

We were passing Hollywood Blvd. and Orange St. when a particularly bosomy blonde smiled our way and opened her black leather jacket, allowing the cool night air to bathe the considerable fullness of her naked breasts in the yellow light of a nearby Hollywood street light. Being professionals ourselves, and City employees at work, we quickly swerved to miss the oncoming traffic, returned to our assigned lane and rolled down the windows to unfog the front windshield.

Business was bad, and all the stops had been pulled out. The women did their best to advertise their wares while keeping a look out for some unmarked police car. Another group of tight skirted loose women bent over and aimed their rears at us as Miss January faded from the rear-view mirror.

Our radio came to life with the dispatcher asking, "Rescue 82 your location."

"Hollywood and Bronson" I replied.

"Rescue 82 a person down, *The Sunset 300*, room 38, incident 364, time out 1935, OCD clear."

If the walls of the *Sunset 300* could speak... they would mostly moan.

We passed a few business women near the coke machine who were busy closing some deals and preparing to open others. The door to room 38 was half open, and we could see our patient as we approached the doorway. "Hello, are you O.K.?" I asked the blonde sprawled on the bed. No answer.

We entered the room and quickly conducted a room to room search to make sure the scene was safe. We knew how to do it since we had both studied old *Miami Vice* reruns during some downtime at the station. My partner covered me, scissors drawn, as I kicked the bathroom door the rest of the way open. Nobody was in there, and there were no other rooms, so we were forced to abandon our police work and turn our attention to the scantily clad and sprawled out blonde.

I touched her shoulder. "It's the Paramedics; we need to talk to you." I tugged a bit on her smooth, bare, pale white shoulder and rolled her over on her back. She moaned dramatically and swept the hair from her eyes. I asked again. "Are you all right? Somebody called 9-1-1 because they thought you were sick. I need you to open your eyes and talk to us." She let out another dramatic, and louder moan; then a series of deep sighs, then a tear, then a quivering lip. She still hadn't opened her eyes or spoken to us, but my partner and I had already come up with several possibilities.

There were several beer cans on the night stand, and a black short hair wig on the floor. A large rubber sexual device was on the floor near the wig next to a handful of condoms, one used.

The light from the bedside table lamp cast a bright glow across the *woman's* face. I looked closer. "Hummm" I said, as I tugged at her long golden disheveled locks. The sandy brown hair beneath the wig, along with the beginnings of a 5 O'clock shadow clinched the diagnosis.

It moaned again, and pulled its blondeness back into place.

After administering a series of painful stimuli, County approved of course, and observing appropriate, even aggressive responses, but still not getting 'it' to speak or open its eyes; we decided to resort to the *definitive* stimulation technique to arouse our patient.

I think it was on the same *Miami Vice* episode where we had learned the room to room search, that I got this technique. I went to the bathroom, filled a plastic hotel cup with water, returned to 'Its' side, and flung the cold water onto its face.

It gasped and sputtered and rapidly flapped its long glued on eyelashes. "God Damn you!" it said.

"Hi, we're the Paramedics; somebody thought you were sick or hurt and called 9-1-1, are you all right?"

"God Damn you! Get the fuck out of here. I don't need you, you asshole!"

Well *it* calmed down a little and my partner was able to take its vital signs, ask a few questions, and determine it was alert and oriented with no medical complaints or injuries.

It wasn't talking to 'me'. I told it we were glad it was all right and said "Good-bye."

"Fuck you!" it called out as we cleared the doorway, and a muffled "Fuck YOU!" to me again as we neared the Coke machine.

"A happy customer?" one of the business women called out as we passed.

"We try to leave em smiling" I snapped back. "I think we've been watching too much T.V." I said to my partner.

"I love Miami Vice" he said. "Let's get some dinner during the commercial."

Chapter Fifty-Eight
I almost forgot

I'm sure there's a *bunch* of things I forgot to put in this book; things that mattered to me, but maybe not so much for you. But I just remembered this…

Hector, my partner and my friend.

He'd gone to the eye doctor and came to work one day and told me he'd been diagnosed with *Retinitis Pigmentosa*. (Which I'm told is one of the leading causes of blindness in young adults.) A short time later he was told he couldn't drive an ambulance with his vision problems, which meant he couldn't be a Paramedic.

Hector told me he didn't understand how I could see where we were going at night, and that he'd follow me closely since he could barely see in the dark. Loss of night vision is one of the symptoms. We were in the ambulance one day, Hector was driving, and the light had just turned green and Hector started to go. I yelled out "Stop!" and luckily, he stopped right away, since he hadn't seen the two pedestrians crossing the street in front of him. Loss of peripheral vision is another of the symptoms.

I mention this because sometimes we get used to our *malfunctions*, and we don't realize things are not as they should be, we just live with the changes, we adapt. If you think something isn't right make sure you see a doctor, don't just accept as 'normal' something that isn't.

Luckily the Fire Department allowed Hector to transfer to the billing unit, and I think he actually enjoyed it there.

On this same note. I teach an EMT class now. A girl in my class once said she often woke up in the morning and the right side of her body was numb, almost paralyzed, but then it got better after an hour or so. It had been going on for years. I asked her if it was like 'Pins and needles' like sleeping on your arm funny or something like that, and she said no, it was like being paralyzed. She thought that happened to everybody. I told her *"No, that's not normal, see a Doctor about that."* So, in case you're having rectal bleeding or something similar, IT'S **NOT** NORMAL.

I recall two incidents that made me think, WTF!

As EMT's and Paramedics we're trained to recognize signs and symptoms of medical problems and to treat them. But sometimes, when we're away from the job, we treat friends and family *differently*. At work, we might tell a mother to take her child to the Emergency Room to have that little cut properly cleaned and looked at by a Doctor. Off duty we might tell the neighbor, "Wash it really good and put a Band-Aid on it."

There was an incident where a retired firefighter was at the Fire Department Credit Union. He saw some old friends there in the parking lot. They were all talking, the others were still working firefighters. As they talked, the retired guy started to look pale and got all sweaty. To make a long story short, they all knew something was wrong with him, but they didn't *insist* he go to the hospital. He died the next day. If that had been a patient with those signs and symptoms, they would have made sure he was transported to the Emergency Room, right then, immediately. Use your good common sense, and/or training, on or off duty, geez.

A Captain was having all the signs of a heart attack at his fire station. The other firefighters called for a Rescue Ambulance, and my partner and I arrived to find the Captain pale, cool, sweaty, and shocky; but his fire crew kept him sitting up in a chair (they should have laid him down) and they didn't give him any oxygen. What the hell? Maybe they didn't like that Captain.

Don't kill yourself, but.

I found it very strange when I became a paramedic, that most of the hangings I responded to were people who had tied something around their neck, attached it to something at eye-level or lower, like a door knob, or a clothes pole in their closet, and then just kneeled down to choke themselves to death. Strange. I'd have gotten a rope and ladder, or maybe would have built an elaborate 'gallows' with thirteen steps. That's just me. There's also this whole *'Auto-Erotic Stimulation'* thing, where people try to hang themselves 'a little' for some sexual gratification, but *accidentally* kill themselves. I'd responded to a couple of calls with young men kneeling down with something around their neck attached to a door knob, with a 'girly magazine' on the floor, and their penis in their hand. Dead. Geez. Always have a trustworthy partner when doing such wacky, and embarrassing, stunts.

A firefighter was at the fire station putting a new car cover over his car. It required that he cut some cords on it to the proper length. He had a 'box cutter' to cut the strings. It

181

had a retractable blade for *safety*. It was a windy night, he was fiddling with tie-down strings. He put the box cutter on part of the car cover on the hood of the car. The box cutter was open, it had a NICE blade. The car cover flapped in the wind. The blade fell and landed right on his radial artery, blade first. I was on the phone at the fire station, there on the apparatus floor, about twenty feet away. He came up to me and said, "I cut my radial artery" and he proved it by taking away his fingers so I could see it spurt. He was black. After cutting his artery he turned a very pale "*Michael Jackson black*." Which is neither here nor there, but I found it interesting. You can figure out the several morals to this story.

A drunk man was with his drunk friends. He had a cut on his forehead. His friends put a tourniquet on, *around his neck,* to stop the bleeding.

Luckily, they didn't put it on very well. His eyes were a little bugged out when we got there, but he would live. This was the same neighborhood, maybe the same guy, who had checked the water level in his car battery by putting a lit match down the hole. Boom.

A young boy and his friends in Venice went to the roof of a three-story building, and were throwing long strips of aluminum duct tape off the roof, so that it would land on the high-power lines below and *short out*, causing a very bright flash as the aluminum tape *vaporized*.

Warning: Don't try this at home. Anyway, it was great fun for a while, until one boy hung onto the falling tape a *little* too long, and was still touching it as it connected with the power lines. He was walking around in a daze when we got there. He had *nasty* third degree burns, he may have ultimately lost his arm from that injury.

Things change in medicine. Our treatment for cardiac arrest used to be a routine big shot of *Calcium,* and a couple big shots of *Bicarbonate.* Later they figured out that the Calcium was a TERRIBLE thing to do, and that too much bicarbonate, if you didn't need it, was also deadly... things change.

There was a very nice fellow named *Sam*, he lived in South Central L.A. and liked to 'hang out' at the local fire stations.

Everybody knew him. He was in his twenties I guess, maybe older, and had some sort of past brain injury, which caused him to have frequent seizures. We all liked him and made him an Honorary Firefighter/EMT/Paramedic/Chief, etc. He wore the same uniform pants and shirt we wore, sometimes he even stayed all night at the station. He would help us around the station, opening then closing the fire station doors when we got calls, handing us the printout of our calls, etc. The first day I met Sam we were eating lunch at Station 46. Everybody was eating and talking about something when suddenly out of the corner of my eye I noticed Sam begin to have a seizure. He was sitting next to my partner who was sitting next to me. My partner just put out his arm and laid Sam back gently, allowing him to have his seizure, with his head and back on the floor, and his legs still up on the bench seat of the table. Nobody said a thing, the conversation and the meal never stopped, and after about 30 seconds Sam stopped seizing and my partner helped him back up to the table. I think one of the firefighters said, "You

O.K. Sam?" And Sam said, "I'm fine" and that was that. Interesting.

Ok, there's probably more stories to tell, but you get the point, it's always *something*. Last chapter coming up, next.

Chapter Fifty-Nine
If you can't beat em...

In L.A. 'City', back when I became a Paramedic, Paramedics were Paramedics and Firefighters were Firefighters.

It seems like few people realized this. Most people just think everyone at the fire station is 'the same.' Even our own City Council had trouble grasping it. In L.A. 'County' it's different, and has been from the start; everyone there is hired first as a *Firefighter*, then later they ask, or force, some of them to go to Paramedic training. The Paramedics get a big pay bonus, and it's pretty much *required* before you're promoted to Captain or higher that you've been a Paramedic. So, 'volunteers' to train as Paramedics are recruited, often reluctantly.

I was a Director on the Paramedic Union's Executive Board for about five years. We had a basic theme by which we conducted the business of the union; "Patient Care." If we were negotiating for a pay raise, we made sure we pointed out the effects of moral on "Patient Care." If we wanted bullet proof vests we explained that this would allow us to work more effectively in dangerous areas, and thereby offer the citizens better "Patient Care." When we negotiated a reduction in hours of forced overtime, increased vacation days, or wanted a second pair of steel toed boots, it was in some way to improve our level of patient care. It was not only an effective tool, and one which helped us maintain our positive public image, it was the 'real' motivation for the majority of us on the Executive Board. We truly took pride as members of one of the finest Paramedic services in the country. After all it was 'Patient Care' that brought most of our 400+ members into this profession in the first place. We wanted to be *Paramedics*.

So, it became particularly distressing to us on the Board, when the Firefighter union began a serious push to take over the Paramedic union, and to bring all of us, Firefighters and Paramedics, into one big 'happy' family. We knew that was not the best system for the highest level of 'Patient Care.'

It was 1979, during my initial Fire Department training, at what was called the 'Tower' (I guess because there was a large hose tower in the parking lot) that the then Fire Chief John Gerard, gave us a little pep talk. He said *"You are the bastard children of the Fire Department"* and proceeded to tell us how we had better 'volunteer' for overtime work and be good little soldiers, or else. The Firefighters would tolerate Paramedics in 'their' fire stations but didn't like it, he made that clear. He was definitely no *Knute Rockne*, and we weren't exactly ready to go out and 'Win one for the Gipper' after that. That tone was reinforced over the remainder of my career. Although not as blatant, the same attitude persisted, and continues even now in too many EMS provider agencies throughout the country. Firefighters find it impossible to believe that someone would want to 'just' be a Paramedic, and that they wouldn't be interested in training as a Firefighter. That just doesn't compute to many firefighters. So, to the fire department, keeping a system of Paramedics who were full-time Paramedics, and Firefighters who were full-time Firefighters, made no sense. They wanted a system like the County fire department had, where *everybody* had to be a firefighter *first*. You couldn't get hired as a *"just"* a Paramedic in the 'County' Fire Department, and they wanted that system in the City.

The Paramedic union was fighting an uphill battle to retain the Paramedic's union as the representative body for the Paramedics, and to keep the L.A. City system which allowed the hiring of full-time Paramedics who were NOT firefighters. It was clear that the voices of 400 Paramedics would be faint within the 3,000 member Firefighter union. If there was any chance at breaking the 'step child' mold and still maintaining the highest standards of *patient care,* it would be within a united organization of dedicated full-time Paramedics. That was our stance.

Unfortunately, this message fell on deaf ears, the fire department was successful with their 'Tokyo Rose' campaign, and unity within the Paramedic organization eroded. Despite warnings of dire consequences to the citizens, and without any 'guarantees' for the many promises made by fire management, the Paramedic union ultimately gave in to a very vocal minority of Paramedics, and the Firefighter union took control of the City's Paramedics.

Now L.A. City looks a lot like most other big city fire departments. You must be hired as a Firefighter first to enter the department now. That means the place for women within the L.A. City 'Boys Club' has shrunk. Qualifying as a Firefighter requires significant upper body strength to lift ladders and carry heavy equipment. That requirement alone eliminates most 'regular' women, unless they've weight-lifted themselves into a body-builder physique.

Without the 'single-function'* Paramedic position, the place for women in fire departments is mostly relegated to a very few women, who like the idea of doing the job of a firefighter, which is largely a demanding *physical* job full of hot and smelly turnout jackets, heavy ladders and hoses, chain saws, heavy equipment, smoke and heat. *That* job probably isn't very attractive to most women, and never appealed to *me*; I liked the job of the *Paramedic*.

In L.A. and other fire departments where they have blended the Firefighter and Paramedic roles, the overall expertise of Paramedics has declined, as the Paramedics promote to higher ranks and *out* of field Paramedic care. The loss of this expertise, and the resulting decline in patient care, is what the Paramedic union had hoped to prevent. Part-time Paramedics, and part-time Firefighters for that matter, result in lower performance in *each* function. A study in the L.A.F.D. showed that.

Well, it was good enough for Johnny and Roy forty years ago. It's amazing how a few good sound bites, and cleaver political influence, can make a giant step backward seem forward.

* These days, in L.A. City Fire, the term "Single-function" has come to mean a *firefighter* that isn't also a Paramedic, rather than someone who is "just" a Paramedic. Like L.A. County Fire, you must now start out as a firefighter in L.A. City. here are no longer "Single-Function Paramedics."

Well that was going to be the end, but that's no way to end a book like this...

Sometimes it's good to have a *huge ass*.

The bad guys had the wrong house. The drug dealer who had done them wrong, lived *next-door*, but she answered the door late that night and one of the men pointed a BIG GUN at her. She turned and ran. She had a HUGE ass, and the guy at the door had a .45. He shot her twice and ran away. I think the bullets were *drawn* to the thing, like some sort of guided missiles, how could they avoid it?

We got there to find her on the floor moaning about how she was going to die. We examined her and found two bullet holes in her massive butt. Have you ever watched an episode of *MythBusters*? They often do experiments with ballistic gel, and shoot into it. Well this woman's rear was like two feet of ballistic gel, and those bullets didn't stand a chance, they were just swallowed up in there and didn't hurt a thing. So for all you women with big butts, you're more bullet proof than those *skinny bitches*.

It was New Year's Eve.

We'd gotten the call shortly before midnight and checked the lady out and found some minor complaint; she didn't need an ambulance. But the New Year was coming in, and outside the gunfire was getting serious. This was a bad part of town in South Central L.A. I asked the lady if we could stay for a little while, until the shooting slowed down. She liked the idea, and we watched Dick Clark bring in the New Year with her.

The girl was fifteen, she had a baby.

We arrived to an OB call and the parents at the door were looking pale as ghosts. Seems their daughter had had a baby. They had no idea she was pregnant, she'd just been *gaining a little weight* they thought. The girl didn't seem to know that she was pregnant either. She said she'd gotten some stomach pains around midnight, and then the baby came out. She tied off the umbilical cord with a shoelace, and cut the cord. She washed off the baby and went to sleep with it. She got up at 7 a.m. and told her parents the strange story. The baby was fine.

A Doberman nightmare.

A guard at a housing project was sitting in the guard shack. He worked with a trained guard dog, a Doberman Pincer. The guard was watching TV and the Doberman was sleeping with his head on the guard's lap. The Doberman had a bad dream. He woke up, half-way, and sunk his big sharp Doberman guard dog teeth into the guard's thigh. He didn't want to let go. The guard yelled out several German code words that meant "Let go" or "Stop" or "What the fuck are you thinking!" and finally the dog let go. The dog had a look on his face like, "Oh, oh, I'm in trouble." Moral of the story, don't let guard dogs sleep with their head anywhere near any important parts of you.

Bullet in the mouth.

He parked his car at one of the cheap make-shift parking lots near the L.A. Coliseum. It was only 5 bucks.

Yada, yada, he comes back after the concert and his car is missing. He asks the guy who took his money where his car is. The guy says "Beats me" and they start to argue. The argument gets heated and the 'parking lot guy' decides he should take out his gun and shoot the guy whose car is missing. He shoots him in the face. For some reason he hangs around until the police get there, and he's being questioned by the police as we arrive. The man who got shot is bleeding heavily from his mouth. I look in there with my little penlight and tell him to "Open wide." There it is, I can see the bullet lodged back there in the space where his jaw connects. If he had been just a 'little' faster, he could have caught that bullet between his teeth and spit it out, and said, "Is that all you've got?"

What? I'm fine.

PCP is a potent animal tranquilizer, it also makes humans seemingly immune to pain. A guy was 'dusted' (doing *Angel Dust*, PCP) and was on a second-floor balcony. For some reason, while on PCP, it may seem like a good idea if you are on a second-floor balcony and you want to get downstairs, that perhaps you should just step over the balcony to get there. Well this guy did it, and when he hit the ground he broke both femur bones, (thigh bones) creating two open fractures, with the bone ends exposed. His legs were sort of folded back behind him with the broken stumps protruding. He was trying to walk somewhere when we arrived, on the bloody stumps. It didn't work very well, he didn't get too far, but he felt no pain. He really didn't seem to *mind* his predicament at all.

Shuush-pen-ahhh.

It was a house full of Armenians. A girl was having some sort of problem and a dozen family members were all gathered around speaking in Armenian and fanning her, putting wet towels on her forehead, slapping her face, patting her hand, etc. It was noisy. I couldn't get the people to quiet down. I turned to a young boy, maybe 12-years-old, and asked him how to say "Be quiet!" in Armenian. I can't remember exactly what he told me, but I think it was something like "Shuush-pen-ahhh." (While writing this book I tried to Google an English to Armenian translator but what I got didn't sound *anything* like that.) Anyway, I yelled out "Shuush-pen-ahhh" and the whole room went quiet. Sometimes I wonder if that smart-alecky kid had me yell "I'm wearing panties!" or "Shut the *fuck* up!"

Whatever it was, they shut up.

~

Ok, there's more I'm sure, but at some point, people *don't* want to see your home movies, and people can only take so many *war stories*, so *I'll* shut up.

Conclusion

So, that's my story. It's one that all of us in the business could tell. The details would vary a bit but the story is the same, it's a tale of doing our best, sometimes saving a life, coming home tired, and of having the *honor* to be the one to answer that call for help.

I'm still a licensed paramedic but I don't 'do' it anymore. It was the job that filled much of my life. My children were born then, and my marriage ended as my career as a paramedic ended.

My youngest daughter remembers me mostly as a dad at home; we were able to adjust our schedules so that a parent was always home with the kids when they were little. There are some memories of me as a Deputy Sheriff. But to my children, I'm mostly a *teacher*. I teach EMT's. I've been teaching now longer than I was a Paramedic. I try to teach the students in my college class that there is more to the job than what they see on television, or what they *imagine*. I make the point over and over again that it's about *patient care* and taking care of *people*. I remind them that the patient may be filthy, the patient may curse at them, the patient may repulse them, or grate on their sensibilities or morals, but that they are *your patient*, and we always give them the highest level of care, the same care we would give to someone in our own family. I hope that advice sticks with them and echoes back to them some day when there are tempted to do less than they should.

I'd like to end by saying that the public is in good hands, and that systems delivering prehospital patient care are devoted to the highest levels of patient care, but I'm not sure about that. Too many of those in charge are concerned about the politics of funding and the politics of *control*. Large firefighter unions are often

193

conflicted when it comes to funding issues; whether limited dollars go toward a new ambulance or a new fire truck; 80% of what "Fire Departments" do are 'Medical' responses, *not* fires. The movement to eliminate dedicated full-time paramedics, in favor of dual trained firefighter/paramedics, dilutes the expertise of *both* positions. A full-time firefighter is a better firefighter, and a full-time paramedic is a better paramedic. That point is arguable, but the logic seems clear.

Across the United States it really is a time warp, as far as patient care is concerned, and in the delivery methods of prehospital emergency medical care. Johnny and Roy could get a little hair dye and take up where they left off, some forty years ago. Most cities still run their systems like that, with part-time paramedics/part-time firefighters delivering the paramedic care and responding in pickup trucks unable to transport their patient without another company to provide transport.

Debates as to the propriety and efficiency of part-time paramedics vs. full-time paramedics will be one-sided. The firefighter unions are well-funded political machines that can pull the right strings to keep the status-quo in place. We can only hope that those who become trained as paramedics within fire departments do so for the right reasons, *patient care* not promotions.

For the most part, we can rest-assured that when we call 9-1-1 those EMS providers who arrive *will* give you the best care possible, as if they were caring for a family member. They will answer your call for help and will give you their *all*. That's what most of us try to do. That's why we took the job.

Lance Hodge

Other books by Lance Hodge...

The Poison of Political Correctness
ISBN-10: 1514166488   ISBN-13: 978-1514166482

A Paramedic's Guide: Wilderness First Aid
ISBN-10: 1500182664   ISBN-13: 978-1500182663

A Kid's Book of First Aid
ASIN: 1503361039   ISBN-13: 978-1503361034

Lost in the woods: A Children's Survival Guide
ISBN-10: 1503264920   ISBN-13: 978-1503264922

The Common Sense Guide to: Dealing with the Police
ISBN-10: 1514339579   ISBN-13: 978-1514339572

Secrets of my Grandfather: A guide to Life's Wisdom
ISBN-10: 1495204642   ISBN-13: 978-1495204647

Available at **Amazon**, Booksamillion, Barnes & Noble, and other fine book sellers.

Made in the USA
Coppell, TX
02 December 2019